100 TESOL Activities for Teachers

Practical ESL/EFL Activities for the Communicative Classroom

Shane Dixon

100 TESOL Activities for Teachers
Copyright © 2016 by Shane Dixon

All rights reserved. No part of this publication may be reproduced, stored in or introduced into a retrieval system, or transmitted, in any form, or by any means (electronic, mechanical, photocopying, recording, or otherwise) without the prior written permission of the copyright owner. Dramatic works contained within this volume are intended only as reading material, and their inclusion does not imply the granting of performance licenses, which must be arranged through the author.

Edited by Dorothy E. Zemach. Book design by DJ Rogers.
Published in the United States by Wayzgoose Press.

ISBN-10: 1-938757-20-3

ISBN-13: 978-1-938757-20-4

Table of Contents

Introduction 4
Part I: Common TESOL Activities 5
   Top Ten TESOL Activities 6
   Reading Activities 13
   Writing Activities 18
   Listening Activities 23
   Speaking Activities 27
   Vocabulary Activities 32
   Icebreakers 35
Part II: Lesson Planning Activities 39
   Warm-Up Activities 41
   Objective Discussion 48
   Presenting Instruction/Modeling Activities 50
   Guided and Less-Guided Practices 57
   Independent Practices 61
Part III: Templates/Activity Resource 65

Note: Activities are sometimes accompanied by a printable template.

A printable template is indicated when you see this icon next to the activity:

Introduction

This manual is intended to help give prospective and current Teachers of English to Speakers of Other Languages (TESOL) some of the most common TESOL techniques and strategies recognized and used in the field.

The manual is intended to be practical, and these techniques, for the most part, follow the general need to communicate, interact, and make language come alive in the classroom. Thus, it would be appropriate to state that this manual is aligned most closely to the communicative approach. This is not intended as a pedagogical handbook nor does it attempt a discussion of research-based activities, rather, it simply highlights common practices in the current TESOL classroom. Practitioners are, however, highly encouraged to seek out studies that demonstrate the utility of each and all of these activities both individually and collectively.

The manual is organized into 3 distinct parts.

The first section introduces teachers to some of the most common activities known in English language teaching, starting with a "top ten" list. What follows are subsections categorized according to the "four skills" of reading, writing, listening, and speaking.

The second section provides insight into a particular model of lesson planning. This model is the author's alone, although similar models are found throughout the ESL/EFL world. The reasoning behind this model is rather simple. A teacher who can prepare a classroom with organized routines each week is more likely to have success. I have also found that my lesson plans are shaped much more readily when I remember certain steps that I might otherwise forget (take, for example, the need to introduce a theme with a warm-up).

The third section includes printable worksheets that demonstrate realizations of the activities described in the manual. Teachers are free to distribute and copy these for classroom use.

I hope you enjoy this small contribution to language learning. May you keep searching for activities that resonate with you and your learners! Any inquiries into this manual can be done by emailing the author at sydixon@hotmail.com.

Happy teaching!

Dr. Shane Dixon
Arizona State University, Spring 2016

Part I: Common TESOL Activities

The most common TESOL activities in the modern classroom are quite different from those of a generation ago. As the communicative approach has grown in both research and pedagogical approach, teachers have continued to discover ways to make the classroom a place of excitement and learning.

The following activities were chosen not only because they are common to the field, but because they elicit the kinds of language production that communicative teachers are looking for. These activities tend to cross over the range of student possibilities, meaning that activities can be adapted for all students, from beginning to advanced, and from children to adults. This does not mean that every activity is necessarily an appropriate activity in the context that you find yourself. However, by reading through these activities, you are encouraged to explore how you might use and modify at least some of these activities so that you are more successful in your English classroom.

Top Ten TESOL Activities

1. Information Gap

Information gap is a term used to describe a variety of language activities with one common feature. In essence, an information gap activity uses as its premise the idea that one person or group of people has information that others do not have. Thus, the point of an information gap activity is to have people interact with each other in an attempt to find all the "missing" information. For example, imagine that one student has a map with all of the rivers labeled, but all the mountains are unlabeled. Another student has a map with all of the mountains labeled, but not the rivers. A teacher could invite students to share information with each other in pairs with only one simple rule: students with the river map are not allowed to look at the mountain map, and students with the mountain map are not allowed to look at the river map. They must complete their maps with both rivers and mountains by talking with each other and asking questions. This kind of information sharing is referred to as information gap, and has become a common TESOL technique all over the world.

Here is another simple example. A teacher assigns 10 questions on a piece of paper to student A. Student B is not allowed to view this paper. In contrast, student B is given an article that contains all of the answers to the 10 questions, but student A is not allowed to view the article. Thus, for students to successfully answer all the questions, Student A must ask Student B the questions, and Student B must report those answers to Student A.

Throughout this manual, you will find variations on information gap in order to stimulate conversation. For example, particular information gap activities are:

I'm Looking for Someone Who...
Interaction Lines
Back to Back Information Gap
Headbands
Reading with Half the Words

2. Classic Jigsaw

Jigsaw is a common TESOL reading activity. There are many variations, but in a classic jigsaw, a teacher divides a classroom into four groups (A, B, C, and D). A reading is also divided into four, with one part for each group (so group A reads Part A). The students in each group must read and take notes on each part of the reading. After each group has finished reading the assigned section, students form new groups, with one member from each original group represented (meaning a member of A, B, C, and D all sit down together).

Students now report information to the members of the new group, and every student should take notes on each section of the reading. This gives students a chance to serve both as a reader, a speaker, and a listener, which naturally encourages interaction. Generally, teachers provide questions that the final group must answer, and should monitor each group to provide guidance and answer questions.

3. Cloze Passage Exercise

The word "cloze" is TESOL jargon meaning "fill in the blank" or "missing information." A cloze passage generally has missing words or phrases in the form of a space (_____). Students listen to an audio clip, either recorded or spoken, and attempt to fill in the blank with the missing information. The cloze passage is a popular TESOL activity because it gives students an opportunity to listen to a popular song, conversation, or topic that uses authentic language students can identify with.

Teachers often hand out a sheet or use an overhead with some of the words removed or altered. The students then listen to the audio and attempt to complete the missing words. A word bank may be provided, and the audio is generally listened to more than one time. Students are then asked to offer the answers that they heard, either individually or in groups. Students in advanced levels can even create cloze passages themselves and, for example, share favorite songs.

4. Journals

Journals are certainly not exclusive to TESOL teachers, but are a powerful way to allow students to communicate at their own speed and comfort, and in a creative and original way. A journal can allow students to express their own opinions, daily habits, lifestyle, tastes and preferences, and so forth. Journals are particularly successful at helping students open up to language as a real opportunity to share ideas, engage in critical thinking, or demonstrate a particular language function (For example, if you wanted learners to use the past tense, you could use the prompt, "Write about a past experience that...").

Journals are often collected regularly (once a day, twice a week, once a week), and while there is a variety of debate on the matter, a number of teachers find that journals are a time to allow students to explore their ideas rather than to express ideas perfectly. In this light, journals are sometimes not graded in terms of grammatical accuracy, but rather in terms of content. Conversely, other teachers use journals as a way of measuring language output, and students are given writing prompts that reflect accuracy as well as content (Example: Write a paragraph that uses the past perfect. Use vocabulary from the following list.) Those who focus on form should have explicit instructions.

5. Dictation

Dictation may or may not seem like a communicative activity. Dictation can simply mean, "Write down exactly what I say," and for some teachers, this may seem like an audiolingual or rote-memorization technique. However, dictation activities are often still used today to help introduce students to new vocabulary or ideas, and can help students to practice their listening skills. It also can give students a chance to interact if done in groups.

For example, a dictation exercise can be done by instructing students to take out a piece of paper and have a pen or pencil ready. The teacher repeats the utterance (a word, phrase, sentence, or paragraph) a specific number of times. Many teachers I know call out a word three times. It seems to work best if a teacher tells the students that they will have to write down every word exactly the way they hear it.

After students are done writing, each student can confer with a partner or group, and then they can raise their hand to add a word they heard until the sentence is completely written. A teacher may choose to correct students or have other students help if a student makes a mistake. Alternatively, students enjoy helping one brave student, who is asked to write the entire utterance on the board, who then asks the other students shout out possible corrections until the entire class agrees.

Another interactive version of dictation would divide a class into teams, and each would choose a team captain to write down what was heard. The winner would be the group with the fewest initial mistakes.

6. Modified TPR

TPR, or Total Physical Response, was a method of instruction created by James Asher that allowed students to learn language through a chronological event filled with gesture and movement, and gave learners a chance to be silent while observing language.

While few teachers today follow each of the techniques used in this method, a number of communicative teachers still use some of the techniques commonly recognized as TPR. Today teachers continue to use elements of TPR especially when helping students build vocabulary. In short, TPR can be a great way to teach a list of vocabulary words, especially those associated with a pre-reading or listening activity. Here is a possible activity that uses TPR principles:

1) The instructor gives new vocabulary (usually two or three words at a time) and demonstrates actions that help to determine the meaning of the vocabulary. (For example, a teacher says the phrase "In the morning" and then shows a sun climbing from behind a desk)
2) The instructor delays modeling, using the time between the narrative and the students' reaction to assess how much more demonstration is needed.
3) Once the students are reacting to the "story" without hesitation and with no actions, the instructor moves on to three or more new words but continues to use (recycle) the previous phrases (For example, "In the morning, I woke up," and then later, "In the morning, I woke up, brushed my teeth, and put on clothes.")
4) The teacher starts to "scramble" the vocabulary, meaning that the instructor presents unexpected combinations of the newly introduced vocabulary. The teacher then gives commands with that vocabulary that the students will use. (For example, "Pablo: wake up! Susan: brush your teeth!)

5) The teacher will continue to address different students, varying between different individuals.
6) The teacher then assesses how well the students remember the actions, possibly by having students perform the actions themselves with their eyes closed. (For example, a teacher might say, "Close your eyes. Now, brush your teeth!" and see if students can pantomime brushing teeth.)

While perhaps not a communicative activity in the traditional sense, certainly students are learning to comprehend language and associate it with actions and objects in the real world. To put a communicative spin on it, you might ask students to "be the teacher" and give commands in groups. Or you might ask students to create their own TPR stories and teach vocabulary they are learning.

7. How to Make a Group (Think-Pair-Square-Share and "Assignments")

Communication in a classroom requires teachers to think of ways to divide students into groups. For example, some teachers have students respond to nearly any question using the phrase, "think, pair, square, share."

Think: Students are asked to think quietly about a question.

Pair: Students respond to the question in pairs.

Square: Students respond to the question in small groups (four or more, a "square")

Share: Students respond to the teacher, either by electing a spokesperson or simply by being called upon

While the think-pair-square-share paradigm works for questions, it is less successful at engaging students in projects or larger assignments. For larger tasks, one of the most successful ways to group students in a class is by giving each student a different assignment. In this activity, a teacher assigns students within a group of three or four to a particular position of authority within the group. The positions might include the "leader" (the person who reads the instructions or gets the instructions from the teacher), "secretary" (the student who takes notes for the group), and "reporter" (the person that reports findings to another group or to the entire class).

8. Talking Tokens/Throw the Ball

Many teachers struggle to have students participate in class. One way to encourage speaking is to have students grab a number of tokens. A token could be a small coin, a marble, a piece of candy, or any sort of small item that can be quickly passed out. Each token stands for the amount of times a student will be required to speak. This tends to encourage students to participate and tends to stop those few students who may answer all the questions. You can explain to your learners that as soon as their tokens run out, they are required to listen to other learners.

Another common variation requires some dexterity, and that is to have a number of bean bags, footballs, or other object to throw in class. A teacher throws the object to a student after a question is asked. Then the student answers the question and throws the ball back to the teacher. Alternatively, students could stand in a circle and throw the ball to each other. Whoever catches the ball must answer the question. This keeps students at attention and allows for more interaction.

Variations of this activity found in this manual:

>   *Toilet Paper Caper*
>   *M&M Tokens*

9. Read Aloud or Reading Circles

While this has been called many different names, the basic concept behind a read aloud is to give learners the chance to comprehend a reading by having it spoken out loud either by the teacher, or with a partner or small group. Read aloud activities give opportunities for a teacher to teach different learners a variety of strategies for reading, listening, and speaking. Before a read aloud, learners may be given a sheet of questions to answer, a list of vocabulary words to look for, or another language task. Here are some tips for a successful teacher-directed read aloud:

- a) Choose a story that students love or relate to
- b) Stand in front of the class and have every student open to the same page
- c) Read in a dynamic voice
- d) Pause often and stimulate interest by asking students to predict
- e) Have students read along to various parts, especially exciting or interesting parts
- f) If possible, watch a movie clip version after you have read a particular chapter

Within the technique of reading aloud are a number of excellent teacher techniques. Consider using several of the following each time you do a read aloud:

- ➤ Choral Reading – all participants read out loud and all together
- ➤ One by One and Sentence by Sentence – each person reads a sentence
- ➤ Dramatic Reading – focus on emotions and feelings
- ➤ Physical Response Reading – describe and act out physical actions and movements
- ➤ Paired Reading – each partner reads one sentence and the partners alternate reading
- ➤ The Leader and The Choral Response – the leader reads one sentence and then the large group echoes back that sentence (or the large group might read the next sentence) and then alternate back and forth between the leader and the group reading a sentence out loud
- ➤ Small Group Reading – create small groups and each student reads a sentence in a circle
- ➤ Male and Female Roles or Turns – all the women read one sentence and then the men read the next or take turns reading the dialog for women and for men

- Fill in the Missing/Silent Words – the leader reads out loud and pauses in the sentence for the group to fill in the words that are the focus of vocabulary or pronunciation practice
- Silent Reading – everyone reads a paragraph or page silently and then questions are asked about the reading or vocabulary, etc.
- Listen and Read – participants watch part of the movie and then read the same portion of the story in the book (this is a good review and a way to cover more difficult passages twice for better comprehension)
- Read and Listen – participants read a passage in the book and then review the same part in the movie (this is a good way to focus on listening to dialog, vocabulary, grammar and comprehension)
- Read and Discuss – the leader can ask questions about the reading or how the participants feel about a topic or idea presented in the book or movie
- Read and Write – participants can write book reports or short essays in a class environment

10. Turn ANYTHING into an English Activity

Veteran TESOL teachers are able to take an object, a group of images, an article, or a video and turn it into an opportunity for students to use English. The idea is that any item—even a picture of an apple—naturally invites students to produce language. When given objects or videos, basic students generally describe what they see, while at more advanced levels, students might make inferences or share opinions about the item.

One variation of this activity is called, "3 Things in a Backpack." I generally grab three things that have some personal significance to me (for example: a trophy, a picture, a ticket stub). I will take each one out of the bag and ask students to write or speak as much as they can about it. I might write vocabulary on the board based on what students say. Then I will explain why I chose the object. After I have shared my "three things," I will invite learners to do the same. I have found it is a fascinating way to get to know students.

But this is just one variation. In general, when a teacher finds an interesting item for students to look at or think about, teachers can use reading, writing, listening, or speaking activities to support it. The website www.breakingnewsenglish.com, for example, turns a typical news article into a huge number of opportunities to learn English. The website offers reading, writing, listening, speaking, pronunciation, and vocabulary activities that all support a single article. Truly impressive.

Here are some simple in-class suggestions:

Writing: You can invite students to write down as many words as possible based on the item, or perhaps create a story based on the item, or craft questions for other students to answer about the item.

Reading: You can invite students to do a web search about the item, or the teacher can prepare a reading that explains information about it. A jigsaw or information gap activity can often be created based on any reading the teacher prepares.

Listening: You can ask students to listen to a short passage based on a picture, video, or reading, or, if using a video, perform a cloze passage exercise. Alternatively, students can listen to other learners in the classroom discuss the object.

Speaking: You can invite students to make predictions from a video, or make inferences about an object. You can create a series of questions that students can respond to individually, in pairs or in groups.

You might be surprised at how much students want to describe something as simple as an apple when given the chance and when given supporting activities. Anything can be an opportunity to teach English.

Reading Activities

Reading activities, for a communicative teacher, often involve helping learners know how to read using a number of different strategies. While many of your learners may think that reading simply involves going word by word and sentence by sentence, researchers now understand that reading is an involved process that can be aided by a number of different techniques and activities. Your job as a teacher is to help learners recognize that reading is an elaborate process that might involve predicting, scanning, skimming, and asking questions (to yourself and to others). Having a specific focus can also help to improve reading skills, such as an attempt to focus on general meaning, specific facts, a particular grammatical item, guessing a word in context, and so forth. Please recognize that a teacher plays a significant role in helping learners "unpack" written language through the use of multiple reading strategies. What follows are a few very simple ideas to help stimulate interaction and thought in an English classroom. Notice that the first two activities here are very simple prediction activities.

1. Predict from a Title

Students are invited to read a title of the reading and then predict what it could be about. Give students time to discuss different possibilities, and help them elaborate on those possibilities.

2. Story Guesswork

Students are asked to guess what a story will be about after skimming the first paragraph, looking a series of pictures, or reading a short description of the characters. Guessing a storyline can intrigue students and get them thinking about key vocabulary. Writing key vocabulary on the board can also help their ability to predict and get them thinking about the reading ahead of time.

3. Jigsaw

See *Top Ten EFL Activities #2*

4. Find a Word, Find a Sentence (Board work Scanning)

In this reading exercise, write a definition of a word on the board without the word itself. Invite students to look for the word in the reading that has this particular meaning. This can be done as students are reading, thereby keeping them alert while reading. For more advanced students, you might invite them to look for a sentence or sentences that answer questions you have placed on the board. Board work like this can help students increase their scanning skills and can help students "look" for all kinds of important details. Using these techniques, you can ask students to search for an interesting sentence, a main idea, a sentence that reminds them of a story, a sentence that the student disagrees with, and so forth.

5. Reading with Half the Words (Learn to Guess from Context)

Since many readings offer a number of words students don't know, this exercise can help students realize that they don't need to know every word in order to understand general meaning. This activity also helps students understand the importance of guessing in context. This reading activity is done by removing half of the words of a text, which can be done easily by cutting a story or article in half vertically, or asking students to cover half of the words with another piece of paper. Now with only half of the words visible, students must try to guess or anticipate what the reading is talking about. Often, a series of questions can be asked about the article to help students guess the meaning. After learners have read the article, the rest of the article is revealed and students investigate how well they were able to predict. If done correctly, this can demonstrate to students how well they can answer questions without knowing every word in a reading. As a variation, you can make this reading activity an information gap, giving student A having half of the words and student B the other half. The goal of the activity is always to answer the reading comprehension questions the teacher has created for the activity. Feel free to see a sample version of this in the templates section.

> **Questions 1-2 are based on passage.**
>
> Early scientists believe dinosaurs, like most reptiles, immediately abandoned their hatched young were left to ta themselves. However, the rec group of nests has challenge nests, which contained fossil dinosaurs that were not unbo dence that dinosaur parents a their young. For some time a babies stayed at the nest whil brought back plant matter for stayed at home until they we roam safely on their own.

6. Reader's Outline

Invite students to create an outline of an article or story they have just read. An outline can help students recognize main and subordinate ideas. It also helps to increase memory and gives teachers a chance to assess student ability to identify supporting details. This activity is greatly enhanced when asking one or more students to share their outlines on the board, and then discuss with a class which details might be added.

7. Character Map

A character map allows students to explore a particular character in a story. Either select a character or have students choose a character from a story. Then have them draw a picture of the character and add symbols and details to describe the character's personality, struggles or problems, and physical characteristics. This can be a predictive activity as well, and you can ask students what you hope will happen to the character and/or what they think will happen to the character later on.

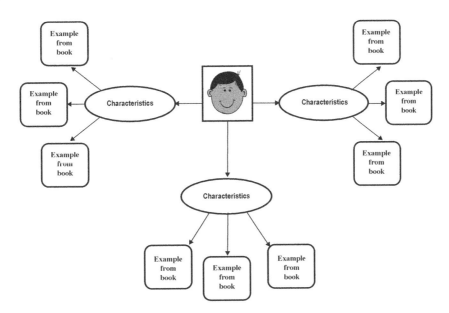

8. Reading Log

A reading log allows students to show what they are reading outside (or inside if you have private reading time) class. There should be a set time each week when students are able to share with each other what they read. They can write down answers to questions, discuss what they liked about what they read, ask questions to others who have read the same book, or whatever you as a teacher would like to have them do in the reading log. A reading log simply means that you invite students to engage in what they are reading. One reading teacher I know uses a reading log to help students use the vocabulary they learned in the reading. This teacher asks students to write sentences using the words they did not know previous to the reading. Another reading teacher I know invites students to write a story based on a minor character, or write as if they were one of the characters.

9. Scrambled Sentences

Several sentences from the reading (for example, 5-6 for beginners, and as many as 10 sentences for advanced learners) are cut into equal-sized strips of paper. Students are required to put them in the correct order either in pairs or groups. For convenience, numbering each sentence (in random order) can help when discussing the correct order.

10. Picture Books

Picture books are a great way to have students relate stories they are reading to each other. Each student is assigned a book or short story to read. Then the student is invited to create a series of pictures (no more than 10) about the story. The pictures are used to give the students a chance to summarize the story to a partner or to the class. If necessary, students may write small sentences on the back of each picture. This allows for students to read and then present on what was read.

11. Focus on Organization

Have students look at the organization of a story. Discuss with them what is contained in the first scene, second scene, third scene, and so on. Then have students retell the story by using words such as first, second, and third.

12. Skits on Reading

After reading an article or story, have students write a short skit based on that story. Students often love to act out the things they have read.

13. Focus on a Literary Technique

EFL teachers can learn a lot from literature teachers. Literature teachers often help teach students about metaphor, simile, symbols, rhymes, color imagery, description, setting, plot, allusion, or other literary devices. Don't be afraid to teach good literary techniques as well as language. It may help students to learn to appreciate the beauty of another language, and will certainly help students to engage in reading.

14. Mapping *(pg. 72)*

Doing a TESOL "Mapp" is especially useful when you are inviting students to look at persuasive writing (such as advertisements). To create a "MAPP", first have students fold a piece of paper into four sections. Second, ask them to put into each of the four corners one of the following words or phrases (usually clockwise starting from the top left): M: Main Idea, A: Audience, P: Purpose, and P: Personal reaction. Finally, tell the students to answer, in the space provided, each of the following questions.

M: Main Idea: What is the reading trying to teach?
A: Audience: Who is this reading written for?
P: Purpose: Why did the author write this?
P: Personal Reaction: Why do you like or dislike this reading?

15. Summarizing/Paraphrase

A summary requires students to take an article or story and relate the main ideas in chronological order. While summarizing is a common activity in some countries, it is not a common practice in others. Thus, teaching learners to condense or summarize information can be an important educational activity. Asking students to find their own words to summarize can be equally challenging, but can help students to learn how to simplify grammatical structures, create transitional words or phrases on their own, and use synonyms for key vocabulary.

16. Picture the Story

In this activity, you can invite students to focus on the location of a story by having them draw what they imagine the neighborhood in which the story takes place. It is often helpful to tell them to think of this story as a "movie": how would it get filmed? What would it look like? This is a particularly good activity for visual learners and those with creative talents.

17. Rank Order Exercise

Have students read and take notes about ideas that seem important (you could ask, "What are the most important ideas/themes from this reading?"). This could be, for example, the main themes of the reading, the morals of the reading, or just a list of the details themselves. It is best if students write full sentences for each item they list (instead of saying, "child poverty" for example, tell students to write, "Children often live in poverty in Brazilian favelas"). Then, after students have created a list of ideas (either on the board or on a piece of paper), give students a "ranking form" (see the Template provided) and invite students to rank, in order of importance, these ideas. Afterwards, you might invite students to share why they ordered the ideas with a partner, a group or the class.

18. Alphabet Reading

While students are reading, write each letter of the alphabet on the board, with space after each letter to write a small response. Then invite students to recall as many facts as they can that start with each letter (For example, "Apricots were John's favorite fruit. Betty didn't like John.") As a variation, provide a sheet of paper with each letter of the alphabet. Individually or in groups, tell students to complete the worksheet. The student or group with the most responses wins.

Writing Activities

Writing activities can come in many different forms. For a communicative teacher, writing activities often represent a chance for students to finally show off their learning and respond to the material presented in class. Thus, writing activities are windows into a learners' mind, giving teachers a chance to assess what students know and think (focus on meaning), as well is how well they are performing (focus on form). These two paradigms, focusing on meaning and form, fundamentally change the kinds of activities teachers create when assigning writing activities.

Those who focus on meaning are generally interested in how well their learners communicate their own ideas, and often spend time creating activities that give learners time to generate, germinate, and expand ideas. On the other hand, for the "focus on form" teacher, writing activities can represent opportunities for learners to follow particular linguistic principles. These teachers often create activities that elicit the proper use of writing conventions or grammatical rules. The activities presented in this section can be used for both paradigms, and often, with just a little imagination, can be used and modified in ways that can simultaneously accomplish a teacher's requirements to pay attention to both meaning and form.

Notice that many of these activities require a teacher to think of a prompt in order to be successful. A prompt can be a question, a statement, or even a picture or object that students must respond to. Writing is often enhanced by the teacher's ability to inspire students to WANT to write, which can be achieved with the quality and interest level of the prompts teachers create. When focusing on meaning, try to ask questions that are all based on a similar theme. This will activate background information. For example, if the class will be talking about the beaches of Hawaii for their next lesson, try to ask 4-8 questions that will encourage students to think about Hawaii (animals, people, food, places). When focusing on form, ask questions that will allow learners to respond to that form. For example, when teaching the past tense, ask learners to describe what they did last week, last year, over the summer, and so forth.

1. Workstations

Place four to eight large sheets of poster size paper on the walls of the room, leaving enough room for learners to form groups. On each paper is a question or prompt that students must answer. Questions might be personal or impersonal, based on a reading or lecture, or even based on a grammatical principle you want learners to demonstrate.

When you create these "workstations," you might want to set up some rules. For example, you might way to require each student to write one sentence at each station, or move in groups to a new station every five minutes. For convenience, you might have students write at their desk first on small sticky notes, and then have them transfer their notes to the posters. Upon finishing the activity, you might ask students to read each thought and star the ones they like best, or you might correct any mistakes or emphasize the vocabulary shared. This is a great activity to get students moving and generating ideas.

2. Free-writes

Free-writing is a technique in which students write continuously for a set period of time without regard to spelling, grammar, or topic. Some writers use the technique to collect initial thoughts and ideas on a topic, often as a preliminary draft to more formal writing. A free write means that students are "free" to write whatever they want, but often you must guide the free-write with a prompt.

3. Fast-writes

A fast-write is similar to a free-write because spelling, grammar, and vocabulary are not evaluated. However, what is evaluated is the number of words written in a given time. Students can gain a sense of accomplishment as they see their writing speed increase. They are generally given an easy topic to fast-write about, and sometimes a teacher will discuss the prompt ahead of time and elicit vocabulary words on the board before the learners begins. For a fast-write to be accurate, a teacher must ensure that the activity is done the same way every time.

4. Brainstorming

Brainstorming is an informal way of generating topics to write about. It can be done at any time during the writing process. Writers can brainstorm the topics for a whole paper or for just a conclusion or an example. The important point about brainstorming is that there should be no pressure to be "brilliant." Students should simply open their minds to whatever pops into them. Think of it as a kind of free association.

For example, with an advanced group discussing poverty and education, teachers might say something like, "When I say 'literacy,' what pops into your mind?"

Much of what the students will come up with may not be useful, but that's okay. Part of brainstorming will involve a selection process. A teacher might write students' ideas on the board, or invite a student to write down the ideas. A teacher can also rephrase questions or add to questions to help students to respond more fully. For example, a teacher might ask, "Is literacy important? Why?" or "What do you think is stopping literacy today?" Afterwards, the teacher might go back to the question: "What else pops into your mind when I say literacy?" As a general rule, when brainstorming with a classroom, expect silence and expect the need for the teacher to follow up with questions. Teachers may also need to call on individuals, or invite students to speak in pairs and groups before sharing in front of the class.

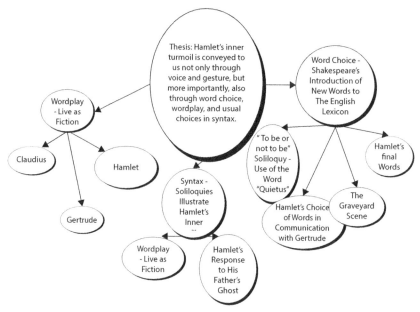

5. Venn Diagrams

A simple Venn diagram looks like two circles intersecting, and is often used as a pre-writing or post-writing activity. Venn diagrams are used to compare and contrast two subjects, objects, people, and so forth. For example, if a class wanted to compare dolphins to sharks, students would place the similar items inside the parts of the circles that intersect (fins, swim, eat fish), and put items that are unique to dolphins (mammals, play with humans) and sharks (sharp teeth, dangerous) in each non-intersecting area.

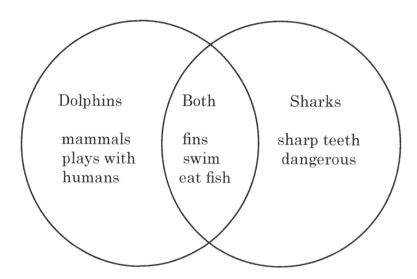

6. Unfinished Stories

Invite students to finish a story or article. This can help them to predict the actual ending, and can also serve to have them imitate the tone and vocabulary of the reading. This activity can be done in groups or individually.

7. Any Four Pictures Make a Story

This activity requires students to think creatively and make connections. It can also be a lot of fun to see how students' imaginations differ. To do this activity, place any four random pictures on a wall (or on a handout). If placing the pictures on the wall, make sure that they are printed large enough for all the students to see. Then have students try to make a story based on those four pictures. Since the pictures are unrelated, the stories the learners generate are usually rather original. Teachers may want to help learners before they begin doing this activity by writing down vocabulary words that they do not know (invite them to ask questions about each picture to generate this list). Other requirements, such as the length of the story and the grammatical elements to be included, should be specified.

8. Guesswork Dictation

In this activity teachers will ask students to write down a few sentences that have been created, as in a normal dictation (see Top Ten TESOL Activities). In this dictation activity, however, replace key words with "impossibly big words" in place of key vocabulary. Have the students write out the dictation. For the large words, tell the students that it is okay to guess the spelling.

(1) Macroseisms happen in Arizona all the time. (earthquakes)
(2) Perhaps not a superabundant number like California, but quite a few. (many)
(3) Flagstaff had the inauspicious honor of three major quakes early in the 20th century. (unlucky)

Share the sentences out loud just like a normal dictation, and allow each student to write down what he or she hears. After, invite students to guess the meaning of the "impossible" word. Students often can remember key vocabulary better when they see a similar, more difficult word, and often enjoy the sound and complexity of larger words.

9. Remember the Picture

Bring a picture that would be interesting for students to look at. Consider a picture with a lot of detail, such as a picture with a lot of people on the beach doing different activities. Handouts can be made for each student or large pictures that can be seen from the front of the class can be used (teachers can even draw their own). Have students study the picture for one minute. Then remove the picture from their sight and have them write as much as they can remember. Students should be encouraged to focus on verbs or nouns, colors or shapes, or whatever language focus is being studied at the time.

10. Draw Your Neighborhood

Have students draw their own neighborhoods. Then have students share stories about their neighborhoods. They might want to discuss a time when they had a fight, their first crush, or other interesting stories.

11. Journals

See Top Ten EFL Activities #4

12. Poetry Writing

Often students are intrigued by different forms of poetry. Teachers can use haiku, limericks, sonnets, and other forms to create engaging writing assignments. One way to inspire learners to write in English is to ask them to produce poetry using poetry templates. A poetry template can help a learner with various kinds of language tasks, and can help to motivate learners to share their lives and opinions. For example, notice this poetry template about "My Hero" that a student could follow to share some information about someone they think of as a hero.

MY HERO

Name
Adjective, Adjective
Noun phrases **(Hint: What Is He/She?)**
Gerunds
Prepositional Phrases

MY HERO
Craig
Calm, Persuasive, Thoughtful
A wise soul, a steadfast rock, a gentle hand
Hearing, Changing, Becoming
Through all of his life.

Listening Activities

The communicative teacher certainly considers well-planned listening activities, and pays close attention to how they are structured and how they will be assessed. The activities listed below will not generally show assessment or evaluative techniques, but rest assured that you should spend time thinking about how you would determine the success of each activity. By thinking of the end in mind, this will help to clarify your language objectives for each activity (in fact, some teachers only have very vague ideas about an objective at all). Remember that a listening activity should not be a "break" in your instruction, but represents an opportunity for students to gain information, skills, and achieve goals. Since listening is generally given at the rate of speed of the speaker rather than the receiver, it can be more difficult than reading, which can be received at a learner's own pace. This difficulty can be overcome as you find techniques to help make listening activities more clearly understood.

Teachers can break down listening activities and lighten the cognitive (learning) load of participants in several ways. For example, the simple technique of repetition cannot be overstated. If students are struggling with a listening activity, consider having students listen more than once and perhaps even discuss or write down what they heard. Another important way to break down listening activities is to pre-teach vocabulary, or to share key concepts ahead of time. Using prediction activities or follow-up questions also help to reinforce the information that students have received. In some sense, a successful communicative teacher is not just one who is able to create strong language activities, but someone that creates a strong support system around each activity that is created.

1. The Missing Half

Divide an article in two, and assign the half of the students to read the first half of the article, while the second half of the students reads the second half of the article. Invite the Student A partners to look for Student B partners (and vice versa). Invite students to read aloud the paragraph to the other partner, making sure the partner does not look. Give each pair comprehension questions (either placed on the board for them to answer on a separate sheet of paper, or a quiz, making sure that questions for Student A writes the answers to questions that relate to material spoken by Student B, and Student B answers questions that relate to material spoken by Student A.

2. Headbands

Place the name of a famous celebrity on a headband, making sure that the person does NOT know what name appears on his or her own headband. For example, if studying a unit on sports, teachers might write a number of famous sports celebrities on the headbands like

Maria Sharapova, Mohammed Ali, or Lionel Messi. Students should walk around the room and look at each headband, with clear instructions not to say the name of the celebrity. The students should take turns asking questions to each other in order to figure out their identity, and instruct students to give helpful clues. This activity can introduce a theme, help students to work on question formation, and give opportunities for students to respond to questions.

3. Back to Back

This is not so much an activity, but a way to do an information gap activity that can be a lot of fun. Students are told to sit back to back: this may involve moving two chairs so that they face away from each other, or perhaps even sitting on the ground with backs touching, if appropriate. Now, in this configuration, give students an information gap assignment with express instructions to never turn around. As in a normal information gap activity, each student must communicate to the other to complete the missing information. This way of doing information gap works particularly well for drawing a picture or completing a map.

4. Quick 20-Question Quiz

Ask learners to write down 20 questions from material they have recently learned (with the question on one side and the answer on the back). These questions are then put into a hat or box. At this point, teachers should review each question and add a few of their own before proceeding to the next step. After reviewing or adding questions, the teacher then selects a question and reads it out loud, and the learners write down the answers. This is a more informal or simpler way of doing a quiz.

5. Truth or Fiction

Instruct students to write something true but surprising about themselves, without revealing it to anyone else. (Example: *I have eaten an entire cake by myself* OR *I have visited twelve different countries*). Tell students that the more unusual it is, the better.

Then, students should write two untrue statements—they can also be unusual, but should at least be plausible so as to trick other students. Then, one by one, each student shares the three items they have written down while the rest of the class members guess which item is "true" of the individual, and which items are "fiction." Upon carefully listening to each truth and lie, class members can then vote which item they think is true and which items they think are fiction. For advanced levels, you can invite class members to ask questions and deliberate in groups or pairs before voting.

This activity can help learners pay attention to not only the words of a speaker, but to tone and body language.

6. Cloze Passage

See *Top Ten Activities #3*

7. Draw a Picture pg. 76

Instruct students to draw a picture, according to the teacher's specific directions. Be sure to have the directions written out in advance, and also have a picture to show students after their attempts at drawing according to your instructions. See the template for an example of a picture with teacher directions.

As a variation, several similar pictures can be placed on a board. The teacher then starts describing one of the pictures. Students should locate the correct picture based on the description. They can do so by raising their hand, writing down the number, or discussing with a group.

8. Perform the Instruction (Fetch It!)

The teacher asks a student to perform a task (generally, asking a student to pick up an item in the room or do something with an object in the room). The other students then attempt to determine whether or not the student did the behavior correctly. Multiple students can also be asked to perform a similar action, such as make a paper airplane. One way to make this assignment more difficult (and fun) is to ask students to listen to the teacher's words (Place your paper on your chair), but then do something different, such as put the paper on a desk. Students who follow the words instead of the actions are rewarded for good listening.

9. Dictation

See *Top Ten EFL Activities #5*

10. Secret Orders

Divide students into two teams. Invite teams to select a team leader and a team performer. The team leader stands closest to the teacher, and all the other students stand in a line behind him. The team performers are the last students in line.

The team leader is the only one who is allowed to see a piece of paper that contains an "order" on it. Orders can be brief or complicated, depending on the level of English of the students (Easy: Stand on one foot. Difficult: Pretend you are a tree falling in the forest because you are being chopped down). The student must verbally relay the message to each person on his team. When the message is finally relayed to the performer, the performer must act out the order.

11. Story with Mistakes

Read a story with students and remind students to listen carefully. Explain that you might make mistakes as you read it (you can say, because I have forgotten my glasses, or another excuse if you wish). Then have students correct you as you make mistakes. Making mistakes that are intentionally funny or foolish can help students enjoy your story reading.

12. Guest Speaker

Invite a guest speaker that might be of some interest to the students. Before the speaker comes, invite students to write down questions ahead of time that they want to ask the guest speaker, and then have students ask those questions during or after the guest speaker's presentation. You may wish to tell the guest speaker ahead of time what questions the students have.

Speaking Activities

Speaking activities have widely been seen as the most demanding for learners. This may be because of the many characteristics unique to spoken language: reduced forms, contractions, vowel reduction, and the use of slang. And let's not forget stress, rhythm, the use of signpost transitions, and so forth.

Speaking activities are also difficult for teachers. In part, this is because even short 5-minute speeches require a significant allocation of time to assess and provide feedback. I mean, truly, how does one observe a student speaking for five minutes without boring the other twenty nine students who are just waiting to give their presentations?

Furthermore, speaking is also difficult to assess since teachers are generally required to create rubrics that contain some of the many possible categories that speaking entails. Teachers must decide: Does speaking include the use of body language? Does speaking include the use of visual aids? These and similar questions demonstrate the difficulty of assigning precisely what speaking, and especially competent speaking, might be.

One simple solution is to simply provide a lot of informal, unassessed speaking practice in preparation for a few more formal events. Thus, many teachers try to get students talking as much as possible, without a focus on formal presentations, but rather a focus on generating ideas, conversing, and practicing certain aspects of speaking.

The activities in this section mostly address this kind of informal speaking; speaking that may not be easily assessed, but allows students to engage in free, open communication practice. However, please pay special attention to the need to create narrow, specific objectives in these activities, and keep in mind that these informal practices should lead to success in a more formal evaluated presentation or speaking performance. Speaking activities, in this sense, take on the very real likeness of practice scrimmages before a big game.

1. Picture Prompt

Invite students to look at a picture and then respond to a partner about what they see. Choose pictures that help students respond to themes or vocabulary that they will need for more formal presentations. You may wish to provide a list of questions for students to respond to while looking at the picture. For example, if you are discussing global warming in class, you might want to show pictures that help students reflect on polar ice, rising sea levels, and animal habitats.

2. This Makes Me Think That...

Students work in groups or pairs for this activity. The activity begins by showing them an article or video. Afterwards, students should begin a discussion by saying, "This makes me think that..." Inform students that each member of the group should be allowed time to think and respond.

After everyone has responded to the material, invite students to respond to each other by using the phrase, "What you said makes me think that..." Tell students that they must continue speaking until the teacher calls the time. This activity allows students to practice continued speech.

3. Circle Speaking

Students should form two circles with partners facing each other (an inside circle and an outside circle, as seen below). Give students a topic or question to speak about. Students on the inside talk first, with the partner directly across listening intently. Students on the outside are then invited to speak, and the partner on the inside circle listens intently. At the teacher's discretion, when students have had enough time to speak, they are required to switch partners by having the outside circle move clockwise (you might want to yell, "switch!" to indicate that students move). When students switch, you can invite switch topics or give differing instructions (now share your idea in only 30 seconds instead of 60, OR Now share what you heard your last partner say). This is a simple game to get students to keep talking.

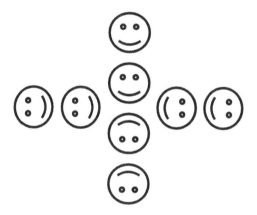

4. Interaction Lines

In this activity, tell students that they will be the "teacher" and will quiz each other. Each student should think of a question that he or she knows the answer to (from a class discussion or a reading). Alternatively, you could provide questions for each student on strips of paper and distribute one question per student.

Now, ask students to line up in two rows and face each other. Students in Row A should ask their questions and the students in Row B will respond. Then Row B will ask their questions and Row A will respond.

After a set time (enough time for each pair to respond), Row A will move one position to the right. The student without a partner moves all the way around to the beginning of the row (see picture).

A simple variation of this game allows students to learn how to narrate. To begin, one row looks at half of a picture or video and describes to the partners facing them what they see. The other row listens to what is being described. Then the partners switch positions so that the partner that was listening is now actively seeing the second half of the picture or video. Then students are brought together to see the entire video or picture, and students are invited to discuss what they could or could not describe. Vocabulary that the teacher overhears can be written on the board.

5. Agree/Disagree Value Lines

Ask students a series of questions that they can agree or disagree with. After students agree and disagree, instruct them to rank the questions according to how much they agree/disagree with each statement using the Value Lines template. Invite students to discuss why they ranked the value lines in that particular order. As a variation, instead of asking students to agree or disagree, you could ask them to love/hate, like/dislike, never done before/done before, or other kinds of classification.

6. Story Chain

Form groups of four students. A student in each group is asked to begin a story. After a period of time (for example, 1 minute) the next person in the group must continue the story. This is done until the story has reached its conclusion or every member has participated. You can begin the story with a prompt that interests students or introduces the theme of your lesson. Tell students that it is fun to leave the story at a moment of suspense. For example: "There was a man who was staring at a bag of chips. He hated these chips. He hated them a lot. This was because…"

7. Folktale Storytelling

Invite students to read a folktale and then recite it, by memory, to the rest of the group. If you have four stories of equal size, you can form groups and invite each member to read their story and share it with the rest of the group.

8. Discussion Questions

While asking questions is a hallmark of every good teacher, it is a very commonly ignored aspect of teacher training. Asking questions to create discussions is an art and a vital skill. Consider the following tips for creating effective discussion questions:

- Ask questions that are NOT yes/no (open ended)
- Ask questions that are "come on" questions, in other words, that are dual sided, but elicit an emotional reaction because you have deliberately made it look one sided ("Technology is bad, isn't it?")
- Ask questions that make students think critically by asking them how they would resolve or respond to a particular problem
- Ask questions and give students time to think
- Ask questions to specific students ahead of time and let them know you will be giving them time in class to answer

9. Fishbowl

This activity requires four learners ONLY to speak, while all others listen. This is done by placing four chairs facing each other in the center of the room (as if in a small group discussion). To begin, invite four learners to sit in these chairs. All other members of the class will sit in chairs in a circle *around* the four students in the middle, thus creating the look of a fishbowl (the outside circle) and four fish in a fishbowl (the four inside students are being observed by those on the outside).

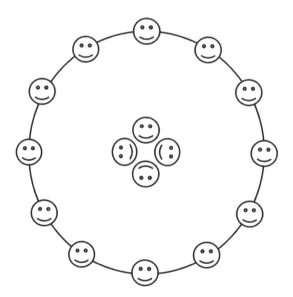

Provide questions for the four students in the middle and invite students to speak at least once for every question. After each have spoken at least one time, other students from the outside circle may take their place by lightly tapping them on the shoulder. This is a good way to spark conversation and allow for students to listen to each other. Many teachers will provide snacks only for those who "enter" the fishbowl. Students on the outside may be required to take notes, and are encouraged to enter when they feel strongly about the conversation. This works especially well for debates or controversial discussions.

10. Three Objects in a Backpack

Place three items in a backpack and explain to students that each of these three things has personal meaning (for example: a trophy, a picture, a ticket stub). Ask students to bring three objects to class and share what the objects mean to them. They should be personal and interesting. The other students in the class should predict what each item might mean before the student shares.

As a variation, hide 3 objects in separate bags. A blindfolded student is asked to feel inside the bag and hold it, but not take it out. The student then must describe what is in the bag to the students. The students must guess what the object is, or write down their answers.

Vocabulary Activities

Vocabulary is often a favorite for TESOL teachers. This is likely because it is easy to give learners a list, and it is easy to provide definitions and give tests. One of the problems, however, is that much of the time vocabulary learning is not durable. This means that students are likely to forget the vocabulary shortly after a period of intense study and test taking. Thus, the best vocabulary activities should help students remember and practice a vocabulary word more than once, and in multiple contexts.

The activities in this section are intended to do just this: help learners use and practice key vocabulary. A number of theorists would agree with the idea that vocabulary must be seen and used multiple times (some say at least 7 times!) in order to become remembered and used. Make sure, as a teacher, you don't commit the unpardonable language sin of teaching a vocabulary word once, and then expecting students to remember and use it.

1. Spaced Repetition (the Leitner System)

Instruct learners to make flashcards and to review these flashcards at intervals or spaces. Tell students that if they answer a card correctly, it goes "one box down" (meaning from 2 to 3, or 3 to 4) and if it is answered incorrectly, it goes "one box up" (meaning from 4 to 3 or 3 to 2). Students are told to study the cards in box 1 every day, in box 2, every two days, and so forth. Thus, incorrectly answered cards are practiced more often, and correctly answered cards are practiced less.

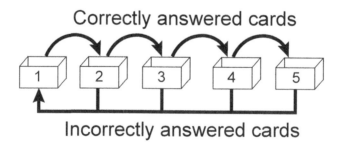

2. Rebus

A rebus strip replaces words with clip art, giving students a chance to practice vocabulary by reading aloud the word every time they see the image.

For example, instead of the word chicken, replace the word with a small image of a chicken and ask students to say aloud the word when they encounter the image.

A rebus strip can be read in pairs or as a group with the teacher. Students can also form their own rebus and read aloud in class.

3. Mix and Match (also commonly called Concentration)

Mix and Match involves having a number of words written on cards, with picture or definition cards that correspond. In other words, if the word on the card is *skyscraper*, you should have another card with a picture or definition of the word skyscraper. It is usually best to have no more than 20 matching pairs.

The words and pictures are randomly placed, face side down, on a board or on the ground. Invite a learner to turn over only two cards, instructing the learner that if he or she finds a matching pair, he or she can continue to look for more pairs. Learners must then remove a single picture or word and try to match it with its counterpart, but if the learner chooses two pictures that do not correspond, they must be turned back over in the precise location. The student can keep pairs that are successfully matched, and the student or team with the most matching pairs wins the game.

4. Collocational Relationships

Collocational Relationships is a game that requires students to find the natural relationships that exist among words. For example, the words *bear* and *honey* could appear on a sheet. The students would be required to draw two arrows between bear and honey. The students then have to consider the relations from bear to honey (with the arrow pointing from bear to honey) and also the relationship from honey to bear (with the arrow pointing from honey to bear). Then students should use words/sentences that make the relationship clear.

Sentences from Bear to Honey:
Bears like honey. Bears are happy when they eat honey. Bears eat honey.

Sentences from Honey to Bear:
Honey pleases bears. Honey gives bears smiles. Honey is a treasure for bears.

The relationships need to be grammatically correct and should demonstrate an understanding of the connectedness of the words, and can also be an easy way to introduce collocations.

5. Jazz Chants

Jazz chants are repetitive mnemonic devices that help students recall information through rhyme and rhythm. Invite learners to clap out a beat and repeat the chant with you. There are hundreds of jazz chants to choose from online, and you can also invent your own jazz chants or invite students to create their own as well.

Say, said.
Stop on red.
Break, broke.
Have a Coke.
Take, took.
Learn to cook.

Eat, ate.
Don't be late.
Speak, spoke.
Tell a joke.
Write, wrote.
Get off the boat.

6. Definition Guessing

Tell students that you will ask them to guess which word from a list of vocabulary you are thinking about. Start this activity by beginning with the phrase, "I am a word that…" in order to create more interest.

7. Flyswatter

Divide students into two teams. Each team is given a single marker and takes turns choosing a leader, who is handed a flyswatter. The leader and group must listen carefully to a definition of a word. A number of words are written randomly across the board. Tell students that the leader must choose the correct word by "swatting" the correct word faster than his or her opponent. The first person to swat the word receives a point for his/her team.

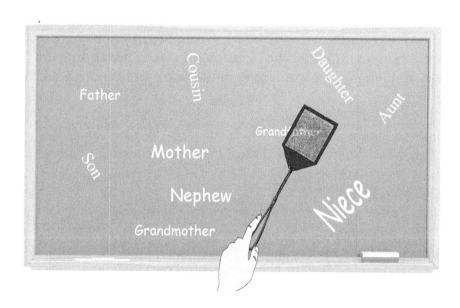

8. The Train

Place students into two groups. Each group must have a row that consists of at least an engine (one student), a car (another student) and a caboose (a student at the end of a row). Instruct students that you will be giving definitions from a vocabulary list they have recently studied. You will then show the definition of a word to each "caboose" and invite learners to transfer the information to the engine. The engine must then write the correct word on the board. The "train" that writes the correct word on the board first wins.

Icebreakers

Icebreakers are activities that help students get to know each other. The term "icebreaker" comes from the idiomatic expression, "to break the ice," meaning "to attempt to become friends." These icebreaker activities are intended to help a teacher, especially in that first week of a class, in order to establish classroom rapport and help students to feel comfortable with each other. Icebreaker activities are essential precisely because language is a skill that must be practiced within groups, and that you must establish groups wherein learners feel comfortable to share, make attempts to speak new grammatical items, and even make mistakes and take risks. Icebreaker activities are also a good idea when a new learner or learners enters a classroom, or whenever you view that learners are not speaking freely with each other. Most icebreaker activities simply have a number of interesting and personal questions, and offer ways to have students stand up and move around a classroom. A good icebreaker generally gets students thinking and moving, and elicits a desire to share not only about yourself, but about other classmates.

1. More Than Name Tags

Use a worksheet like More Than Name Tags to help learners ask about fellow classmates. More Than Name Tags is, in some sense, a giant name tag that gives interesting information about each student.

First, invite learners to write his or her name in the square that is surrounded by four other squares. Then tell students to fill in the other four squares: places, people, things, and dates. You may wish to model this for students by having a name tag that you have created about yourself.

As students fill out their names tags, you may need to help them find the right words for each category. After students have filled out their form, have them pin it to the front of their shirts and ask them to go around and introduce themselves, making clear that they should ask questions based on the four squares. You may need to model questions on the board:

- What places have you lived?
- Who are those people?
- Why did you write down those things?
- Why are those dates important (to you)?

As a variation, invite students to be in pairs, and tell the pair that they will introduce a partner by sharing one or more things that they learned about the person.

2. String Get-to-Know-You

This game requires a ball of uncut yarn and 10 get-to-know-you questions. Invite students to stand in a circle. Instruct the students that they must answer a question if they are holding the ball of yarn. Begin with the ball of yarn, making sure to hold on to the end of the string with one hand, and throwing the ball with the other hand. When the student catches the ball, make sure that you ask them to make sure that the string between the student and you is tight, like a line, connecting the two of you together. Now ask the student one of the 10 get-to-know-you questions. Here is a small list of examples:

- How long have you been studying English?
- What are your hobbies?
- What do you like to do in your free time?
- What hobbies do you have?
- What kind of people do you like?
- What kind of people do you not like?
- What languages do you speak?
- What's something you do well?
- What's your favorite food?
- Do you have any pets?
- Are you married or single?
- Do you have brothers and sisters?
- Do you like baseball?
- Have you ever lived in another country?
- Have you ever met a famous person?
- How do you spend your free time?

The students must then pass the ball of string to someone else, making sure that each person holds the string with one hand, so that eventually the string forms a web. It is fun to watch and fun to catch and is a great metaphor for how we are all connected through language.

3. Find Someone Who (Information Gap Game)

Provide each student a handout (feel free to see the template at the back of this manual). Tell students that they will be "finding someone who" matches the description on the list.

Tell students that you can only have one student sign per handout. Tell students that they must change the prompt to a question. In other words, if the template says, "Find someone who has a short name," then the speaker must ask, "Do you have a short name?" If the speaker asks a question, then the listener can give an answer (Yes, I have a short name. No, I don't). If the answer is affirmative, then the partner can sign the paper. The person that obtains the most signatures is the person who wins the game. This activity requires students to get up and move around, and can be a great way to mix and mingle.

4. Three Objects in a Backpack

Place three items in a backpack and explain to students that each of these three things has personal meaning (for example: a trophy, a picture, a ticket stub). Ask students to bring three objects to class and share what the objects mean to them. They should be personal and interesting. The other students in the class should predict what each item might mean before the student shares.

5. Sentence Starters: What's My Line?

Give students a handout with unfinished sentences and tell them that the entire class will be required to finish one of the many sentence starters listed on the handout. Tell students that you will begin, and choose one of the sentence starters and finish it (For example, "I love to give good students an A in this class." Then choose another student, and choose a sentence starter for them. Juan, what will you never forget? Juan: I will never forget...

As a teacher, you will need to help students to prompt the next student by creating a question from each prompt. At more basic levels, invite students to choose their own prompt. At advanced levels, have students do this exercise in pairs or groups.

6. Value Lines

Tell students that everyone will have to stand on a line in the room, and that the room is divided into two parts. Place signs to help people see the two different sides of the room. Tell students that one side of the room is for people who STRONGLY AGREE, and the other side of the room is for people who STRONGLY DISAGREE. Tell students that they will have to stand in the part of the room that they think most closely resembles how they feel.

Have a few prepared questions wherein students might agree or disagree strongly. For example, "I love sports," or "I like to have a clean room," or "Television is better than reading."

If a student really loves sports, they would stand as far to the one side of the room as they could. Alternately, if they hated sports, they would stand on the complete other side of the room. If they don't care that much, they would stand somewhere in the middle. Tell students that they must talk with each other to decide who agrees or disagrees more or less. Some questions, such as, "I have been studying English a long time," can definitely get conversation going and make individuals have to decide where they fit in a line.

7. Toilet Paper Caper

The Toilet Paper Caper activity begins by standing at the door students enter. As you stand at the door, as students enter ask them the unusual question: "How many pieces of toilet paper do you need?" Do not tell students what the toilet paper will be used for. If a student asks, just tell them (cryptically), "Just take as many as you think you need."

After everyone has entered the classroom, explain to students that the pieces of toilet paper indicate the amount of items a learner must reveal about him or herself.

8. M&M's

This game has the same rules as the Toilet Paper Caper. However, instead of using toilet paper, which is weird (although it can be funny), use M&M's or another small candy to represent the times a student must answer something about him or herself. Tell students that they cannot eat the candy until they have said something about themselves.

9. Venn Diagrams
See *Writing Activities #5* pg. 75

Note: When using a Venn Diagram as an icebreaker, invite students to meet in pairs and discuss things they share in common and things that make them different.

Part II: Lesson Planning Activities

Instructional design varies from discipline to discipline, and there are many models that might evoke a similar look to lesson planning. Nonetheless, this lesson plan design includes some of the most basic elements of instruction that might be of use for the English language instructor. The terms used here are somewhat universal, but other terms exist and, once again, vary from context to context. For example, the term "warm up" is referred to by other instructional designers as a "theme introduction," "attention getter," or as a process of "activating/engaging learners."

1) **Warm Up**
2) **Objective Discussion**
3) **Present and Model**
4) **Guided or Controlled Practice**   } **7) Assessment**
5) **Less Guided Practice**
6) **Independent Practice**

Step #1: "Warm up" or Prepare Students – In this portion of a lesson, a teacher "warms up" the students by activating the students' background knowledge and introducing new knowledge. A teacher may do this by presenting some key vocabulary, eliciting students' knowledge of the subject, using prediction exercises, etc.

Step #2: Discuss the Objectives – In this portion of a lesson, a teacher attempts to give learners a metacognitive understanding of the lesson itself. In simpler terms, the teacher is, either explicitly or implicitly, trying to help students learn WHY they are doing what they are doing, and HOW these objectives, if obtained, might help them. Teachers who engage in these kinds of metacognitive strategies tend to have much more highly motivated students. Teachers themselves also attain better clarity and focus by having the objectives clearly stated and understood.

Step #3: Present Instruction/Model – In this portion of the lesson, teachers give students new information they must know or new skills that they must acquire. Teachers here attempt to scaffold, explain, or otherwise break down information for students to grasp the new concepts. In addition to presenting or instructing, teachers are encouraged to provide models (examples) for students to follow. For example, a teacher might give a sample dialogue, a model essay, or put the necessary vocabulary to be acquired in sentences.

Step #4: Guided or Controlled Practice (Practice #1) – In this portion of a lesson, students are invited to practice their new skills and become familiar and comfortable with it. For difficult language concepts, this practice is often very controlled, meaning that it is done with a lot of guidance from either the teacher or other experts.

Step #5: Less-guided Practice (Practice #2) – Following a controlled practice, students are often given practice that has less constraints and higher difficulty. For example, rather than doing an activity with a teacher, students might be required to do an activity in pairs or groups. In addition, the activity itself might be put modified to provide additional support. A teacher still facilitates learning by answering questions and providing support to the groups or pairs, and the activity itself should help students to gain more comfort with the language required.

Step #6: Independent Practice (Practice #3) – After a sufficient amount of pair or group work, the students are given an independent activity. This often means that the student will work alone to demonstrate the knowledge or skill that they have acquired. This can be done through a quiz or testing scenario, or some sort of performance such as a presentation or written representation of their newly acquired language skills.

Step #7: Assessment – Evaluating student work can happen at any stage of a lesson. *Formative assessment* generally refers to the kind of assessment that is done during instruction, and could include asking questions, giving informal quizzes, and eliciting student participation. *Summative assessment* often follows an independent practice, and is meant to measure a student's ability to attain the objectives set out in the lesson plan. It is meant not only as a measure of the students, but can also provide feedback to a teacher as to how well the instruction was received, and what parts of the instruction need continued support.

This lesson plan template represents a theoretical construct only, and should not be used in a lockstep manner. In other words, novice teachers might be tempted to provide 3 practices (controlled, less-controlled, and independent) for every lesson plan, but this would be a mistake. Some language concepts require much MORE than three practices to attain fluency, and some language concepts might be acquired without any practice at all. Thus, a wise teacher will gauge the amount of instruction and practice needed, and modify accordingly. Since this template is subject to a kind of reductionist abuse, it is highly recommended that teachers use it with the recognition that any and all of these "steps" can be skipped or put in a different order. A one-week template can guide you to consider not only these 7 steps, but using a variety of listening, speaking, reading, and writing activities as you construct a unit.

pg. 81-82

Warm-Up Activities

A proper warm-up activity can accomplish several purposes. First of all, warm-up activities can bridge old to new information, thus leading students to make a connection between previous lessons and a new theme or concept. Thus, in its most basic form, a warm-up activity helps students remember what they know (stimulate the recall of prior knowledge) and then build upon it. A warm-up activity also introduces new information in a way that serves as an attention-getting device, thus, warm-ups are sometimes called attention getters.

That stated, a warm up should not just gain students' attention but direct that attention to an appropriate target, thus it can and should also serve to bring students a broad view of a topic that will be introduced at a later time in the lesson plan more specifically. Good warm ups are ideally intriguing to learners, at least in the sense that they can give information in a way that invites curiosity and elicits prediction activities. Thus, the use of visuals, question prompts on the board, or small videos are common.

Another way to think about warm ups is through the use of the idiomatic expression, "prime the pump." This expression, which means, "to stimulate growth by providing a small catalyst," comes from the old fashioned approach of pumping water from a dry well pump. Water will often not come out of a well pump that is dry, so often a small amount of water is placed in the pump so that it stimulates the pump and provides enough lubrication for that pump to begin drawing water. In a similar way, a warm up is a small activity that "primes the pump." In other words, a little activity, (like a little water), activates background knowledge, intrigues students, and gives students access to all that they know (the well).

Warm ups often naturally lead into objective discussions, which can further inspire students to consider what skills they will gain through the completion of the lesson.

1. Written Prompt on the Whiteboard: Question or Statement

The use of a question or statement can be a powerful way to introduce a class, especially if the English class is theme-based (generally a reading, writing, listening, or speaking class). While the concept is simple, finding the right question or statement to evoke participation is not so simple. When you use this technique, make sure that you are inviting students to respond to something that directly targets the information you will be trying to teach later on. Often, a quote that invites a difference of opinion or multiple angles can stimulate conversation. Using a quote from a famous individual can also invite a discussion about what people know about that individual (What do you know about Martin Luther King,

Jr.?), how they feel about the quote (Do you agree or disagree with this statement?), and can lead into a prediction exercise about future content (What do you think this quote has to do with what we will talk about today?) It can also be tied to past content (What does this have to do with what we discussed yesterday?) In other words, when you write a question on the board, what often follows are a series of follow-up questions to help students start talking and thinking about the theme. Write down words and answers, when appropriate, as students respond, and give positive feedback for those who are willing to speak. While this warm up may only be a few minutes long, it can serve to engage students into thinking about the theme and give you information about what students already know. Consider the following example themes, and sample prompts that might accompany those themes:

Level	Theme	Prompt (Question or Statement)
Basic	Family	What makes a family?
Intermediate	Family	What do you love (AND HATE) about your family?
Advanced	Family	A family isn't always about blood. Agree or disagree
Basic	Food	What are your favorite foods?
Intermediate	Food	"All you need is love. But a little chocolate now and then doesn't hurt." Charles M. Schulz
Advanced	Food	"There are people in the world so hungry, that God cannot appear to them except in the form of bread." Mahatma Gandhi

As a variation, you might provide a written prompt on a sheet of paper and have students respond to it privately as a writing activity, or in pairs and small groups.

2. Pictorial Prompt

While it is commonly stated that "pictures are worth a thousand words," in the TESOL world, pictures *elicit* a thousand words. A good picture can help to begin a class conversation and have students immediately engage in thoughtful discussion. Just as in a written prompt, a pictorial prompt involves a teacher asking a lot of questions about the picture to lead students into a discussion about the current lesson. A good pictorial prompt should be large enough for all students to see, and often has something unusual or interesting to talk about. You may begin by asking, "What do you see?" or ask a more specific question, such as "What problems do you see in this picture?" or "Why is this boy sad?" A good picture often has multiple answers, and a teacher can ask for a wide variety of opinions. When students are answering, a teacher may have to provide key vocabulary to explain certain visual items (Does anyone know what this is? It is called a rainbow. Let me write that on the board). Remember that you may wish to have students write down their answers, or discuss in pairs or in groups before they speak to the entire class or to you as a teacher.

3. Scrambled Sentence Strips

For this activity, you must have a reading in your future instruction. Several sentences from this future reading are cut into equal-sized strips of paper (4-5 for beginners, and as many as 10 sentences for advanced learners). Invite students individually, in pairs, or in groups, to put the sentences in correct order. For convenience you may wish to number each sentence (in a random order), so you can discuss the correct order after students are done. After students assemble the scrambled sentences in order and there is a class consensus on the correct order, ask students what they think the reading will be about, pre-teach vocabulary by using the words in the strips, or get students to share their thoughts about what they have read so far. If possible, you may wish to put a larger version on a whiteboard and show the correct order, as in the example here below.

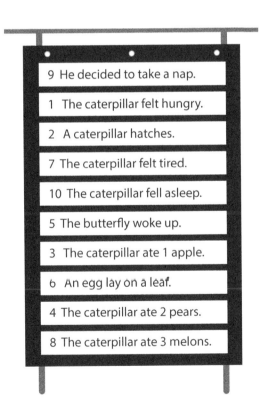

4. Back-to-Back Information Gap: Recycling Vocabulary

This is a vocabulary activity. Eliciting key vocabulary can be a good way to introduce students to a new theme, especially if the vocabulary has been used previously (using vocabulary from a previous lesson is called recycling). In this activity, divide students into pairs. One student will be looking toward the whiteboard, while the other student will have his/her back turned away from the whiteboard. If possible, have student chairs facing opposite direction so that students face back to back.

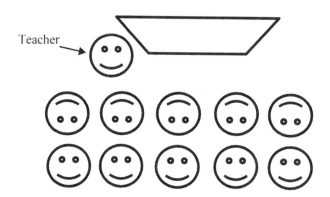

Write 5-10 word or phrases on the whiteboard. Tell students that they must help their partner to guess all five correct words and write down their answers on a piece of paper. The other student can ask questions but cannot turn around. When the student has guessed all five words, the pair can raise their hands. The activity stops when all students have raised their hands or after a certain amount of time that you can decide.

As a variation, you may wish to include words that have never been introduced to students. In this variation, it is important to include words that you believe at least some students know, and, as always, are key words for the lesson plan.

5. Dress-up or Box Props

While this activity can be a bit risky, it also has the added benefit of being one of the most memorable. If you are talking about a cowboy and reading about a cowboy, why not dress up like a cowboy? When performing this activity, you can do several linguistic activities at once. You can ask students about vocabulary and invite them to guess at some of the features of the costume (these are "spurs", this is my ten-gallon hat). You can also invite students to guess what the theme might be. You might also want to act out a small skit to help the students understand some of the upcoming content. While a number of teachers might not feel comfortable putting on a costume, nor have the time and resources to find one, a more feasible alternative is the use of box props. In this activity, bring in a box of items that relate to the theme, pull out each item, and have students discuss each item and then the items as a whole. Sometimes a single prop is all that is necessary to intrigue students and to introduce a theme.

6. Vocabulary Scramble

This is a pre-teaching vocabulary activity. Place a large number of words on the whiteboard in any order (scrambled) and all over the board (you may wish to write some words sideways, some up high, some down low), with a corresponding sheet of paper. Invite students to define the words they know on the sheet of paper. Then invite students to share definitions of each word, and teach the learners the words that they do not know or recognize. Have them write down those definitions as well.

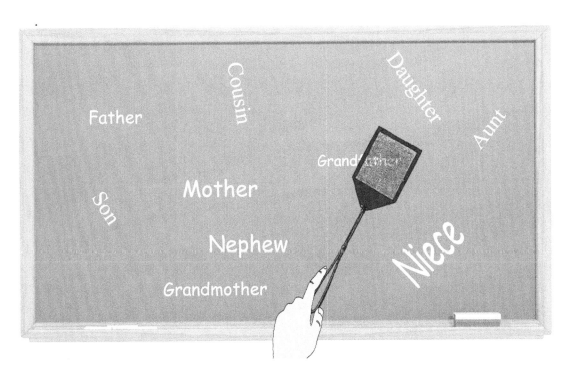

As a follow-up activity, you may wish to do a "flyswatter game." To do this activity, divide students into two teams. Each team is given a single marker and takes turns choosing a leader, who is handed a flyswatter. The leader and group must listen carefully to a definition of a word. A number of words are written randomly across the board. Tell students that the leader must choose the correct word by "swatting" the correct word faster than his or her opponent. The first person to swat the word receives a point for his/her team.

7. Warm-up with Dialogue

Invite students to listen to a dialogue. The dialogue can be performed by two students, by you and a teacher, teaching assistant, or student. Tell students to listen carefully for key vocabulary and ideas. Have students summarize the dialogue on a separate piece of paper, then ask students to respond to the dialogue. As with all warm ups, the dialogue should include key vocabulary and themes for the lesson, and should invite students to think, talk, and predict.

8. Idiom Madness

In this activity, introduce the theme or lesson by using one or more idioms that relate to the theme. You might place them on the board or on a sheet of paper. Invite students to respond to which ones they have heard of, which ones are new to them, and how they might use such idioms. Then invite students to think, talk, and predict the theme for the lesson.

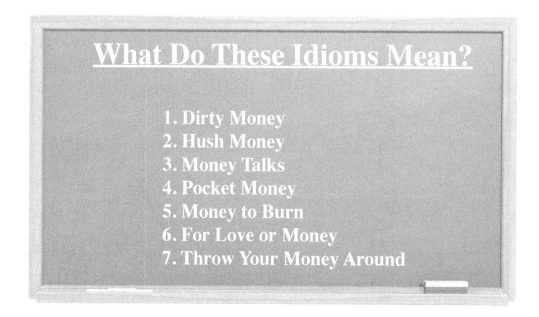

9. Ranking Activities/Value Lines

In this activity, you will ask students a series of questions or statements that they can agree or disagree with. For example, for a theme on food, you could have a number of prompts such as:

Do you love broccoli?
Do you love ice cream?
I eat a lot in the morning.

I want to eat better.
I eat when I am happy.
I eat when I am sad.

There are several ways to have students show their agreement or disagreement. First, you could simply have students hold up a thumbs up or for agree, or a thumbs down for disagree. You could also have them hold up different colored paper (for example: green for agree, red for disagree). Another way to have students rank the questions is by having value lines. The advantage of the value lines is it allows students to strongly agree or disagree, or perhaps give a neutral answer.

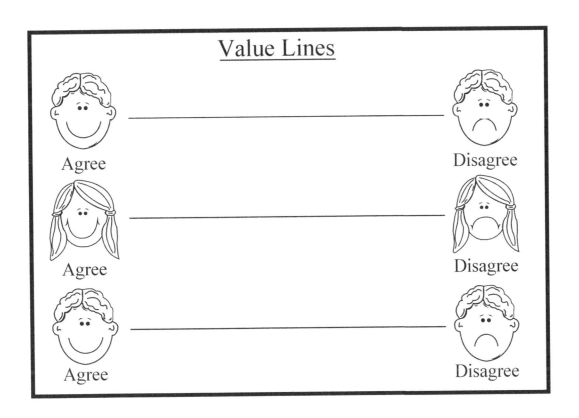

Perhaps the most interactive way to have students agree and disagree is by having them line up as a classroom, often against a wall (as shown below). In this variation, show students that one side of the wall stands for agree (you might want to place a happy face or some other symbol there), and the other stands for disagree (place a sad face on that side of the wall). Explain that if you are in the middle of the wall, it means you neither agree nor disagree. Then invite students to line themselves up according to each question you have given them. Questions such as, "I was the earliest person to eat breakfast this morning," will cause students to carefully discuss with each other and create a lot of interaction and discussion.

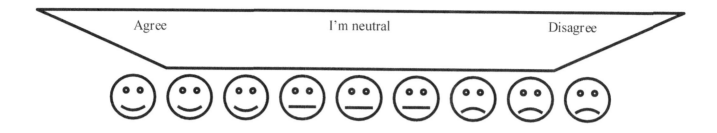

Objective Discussion

An objective discussion is a fairly simple concept. Students tend to perform better when they are told WHAT they are doing and WHY they are doing it. Thus, a teacher that is able to clearly convey the trajectory of the lesson plan is more likely to have students aim correctly toward that trajectory. Metaphorically, it is like teaching how to use a bow and arrow: teachers point to a target they want students to hit. In this somewhat simple view, it is understood that students are better able to hit what is clearly pointed out to them. Thus, an objective discussion is an opportunity to give students an understanding of what the goals for the class might be. In general, an objective discussion entails what learners will be doing (the activities of the day) and what they will be able to do by the end of the instruction (the skills they will acquire).

For some, it is surprising to hear that an objective discussion can be held at any point in a lesson. While it is traditionally seen at the beginning of most ideal lesson plans and lesson plan templates (as it is here), there can be good reasons to hold off to have a detailed objective discussion. Some learners, especially in compulsory situations (such as a mandatory English class in high school) may assume that objectives of the class are out of their control, and thus resent being told what they will be doing and why. The general goals of the instruction may not, in fact, be their goals. In certain cases, such as the one just described, some objective discussions can be held with more success if students already begin to see a certain amount of progress, and thus perceive that they are being led down a path that they want to continue to pursue. In these cases, it is wise to wait until there is initial success to invite students to join in the goals you, as an instructor, have for them. Furthermore, some learners simply perceive that you, as the professional, know what you are doing, and thus don't care what objectives you may have. Think of it as a pilot telling you on a plane flight HOW he is going to get to the final destination. As Jerry Seinfeld once said, "Fine. Do whatever you want. Just get us to where it says on this ticket." In an English class, your overarching goal, get students to understand and speak English, is simply assumed by most learners.

But for an idealized situation, there is no doubt that sharing objectives BEFORE a lesson plan is sound advice. Most learners in most situations want to know where they are being led, and learners tend to do better when they are given a target to aim at. Learners also, with a good objective discussion, can set their minds and hearts to have your goals become their own. Thus, an objective discussion can elicit a certain amount of motivation in learners, especially if an instructor knows how to "sell" the skills that the learners may acquire.

Generally speaking, you may achieve better results in an objective discussion by:

1. Clearly stating the instruction, including subtasks (You will be able to answer a phone call that includes a greeting, a request for help, a display of information, and a closing statement…all in English!)
2. Checking for understanding (Tell me, in your own words, what are the parts of a normal phone call? What do you do when you answer a call? Do you use these four things I wrote on the board?)
3. Discussing the importance of the objective (Why would you like to learn how to speak on the phone in English? Why might it be important to answer a phone call?)
4. Establishing specifics (You will be required to identify and use 15 new phrases in a speaking test tomorrow wherein I will call each of you on these two phones.)

Notice that when discussing the importance of the objective (3), it may be best to ask probing questions to get answers from students rather than just telling them what is important. This is done to ensure that students identify with the goals and see their own importance, rather than simply being told that the objectives are important.

Also, remember that as you write your own objectives, whether they are shared with a class or not, it is important to have specific objectives. An objective is a clearly defined goal that can be measured, generally demonstrating something that a student can do (thus, observable and measurable), rather than something a student knows (something that cannot be observed or measured). Thus, action words such as identify, state, recognize, and demonstrate are preferred to more static verbs such as know, believe, feel, and understand.

This manual does not include activities for an objective discussion, per se, rather invites you to think about when and how to include one in your lesson plans.

Presenting Instruction/Modeling Activities

The phrase "presenting instruction" means a lot of things to a lot of teachers, and how to present instruction is certainly the subject of some debate. For many traditionalists, presenting instruction means giving a lecture or presentation. However, in today's world, and in the world of the communicative classroom, presenting instruction can represent much more. Besides lecture-based instruction, teachers in today's world might present instruction as a problem to be solved (problem-based curriculum) or as a case study or live experience (experiential curriculum). Information might be presented online or without the use of a teacher initially, as is the case in some flipped or blended learning environments. Regardless of the activities employed, presenting instruction represents an initial contact learners have with new material. That initial contact is generally enhanced by the teacher in some ways. For example, a teacher might employ a number of visual aids, repeat key information, provide clear board work with examples, and so forth. A teacher might also use the instructional period as an opportunity to tease out questions and comments from the learners, creating a critical thinking environment that provides a chance for the teacher to elaborate, clarify, and improve learners' initial understanding.

Next to instruction is modeling, which refers to the use of clear illustrations and examples for learners. Modeling activities, in their basic conception, require a teacher to demonstrate or show the task that the students will be asked to produce in the future. Thus, modeling activities involve either a live teacher demonstration of the future task or some previously created model from outside the classroom (past student work, a teacher-prepared sample). When teachers are interested in having students perform a difficult writing or speaking assignment, a model with clear steps is imperative. Some comprehension-based theorists have demonstrated that good models lead to noticing of features in daily language input, and thus are prerequisite for learning to occur.

1. Teacher Talk

Teacher talk is not so much an activity as it is a variety of skills that, in some sense, refer to the craft of instruction itself. Teacher talk refers to the ways in which a teacher involves students through the use of repetition, reduced linguistic forms (especially for basic students), enunciation and pacing, changes in tone, the use of body language, signpost expressions, and other techniques that deliberately modify and/or simplify communication. In general, when you present language instruction, think about key words you may need to modify or define, key phrases to repeat and write on the board, and ideas to elaborate or clarify. Teacher talk is a skill that often involves having an intuitive feel for what students will likely respond to and struggle with, so teacher talk is an activity that comes more naturally with deliberate planning.

Repetition: Repeat key ideas. Place them on the board. Define the most difficult words.

Reduced Linguistic Forms: Look at your instruction and identify difficult phrases and concepts. Find synonyms or simplistic phrasing to replace or amend these difficult phrases and concepts.

Enunciation and pacing, changes in tone: Speak clearly, and vary your rate of speech. Words and phrases that are particularly important or complex are given more time. Do not speak monotone, but vary your tone to match the material (engaging, probing, inquisitive, delightful, serious, etc).

Use of body language: use your body to convey different ideas such as a change of topic, a difficult point, a visually interesting phrase, an action, and so forth.

Signpost expressions: Use clear signal words to help students recognize shifts in organizational patterns. First, second, third, finally, but…

2. Story and Metaphor

The use of story and metaphor can work very well in language instruction. That said, stories and metaphors can be particularly problematic if they are not clearly presented. When used correctly, these techniques are especially effective in helping students recall information, and are also effective at eliciting a response or an emotional reaction from learners.

Imagine that a teacher wishes to give instruction on the simple past, present, and future tenses. This teacher especially wants to demonstrate their characteristic differences. This creative teacher might, therefore, invent a story, one about Mr. Past, Mr. Present, and Mr. Future. The teacher might demonstrate that they are all similar in some ways (they all love verbs) and share a story about how each man behaves when he sees a "cute little verb" on the side of the road while out for a ride (verbs are represented by cute little animals). Mr. Past owns an old truck, Mr. Present has a shiny new sports car, and Mr. Future has a futuristic-looking motorcycle that can fly. The teacher might explain that while each man picks up the verb, each does something different. Mr. Past, for example, takes every verb he picks up on the road and puts two shoes on the verb's feet, *size e and d*, and then puts each verb in the *back* of his truck. Mr. Present also loves to pick up verbs while driving, but he puts them beside him in his convertible and shows them off to everyone as he passes. He doesn't put shoes on a verb, unless Mr. He or Ms. She is traveling with him, in which case he lets Mr. He or Ms. She put a *size s* shoe on the verb. Mr. Future, on the other hand, when he picks up a verb he hangs it in front of the wheel (will) of his motorcycle like it is an ornament. Mr. Future always hopes that his girlfriend notices the verb when he gets home. For Mr. Future, the verb is always placed in front of the wheel (will).

This is a silly story, no doubt, and one that might need some visual aids and some diagrams to make it work, but it is one that students are likely to remember. Again, be careful, all metaphors and stories go wrong when investigated too closely, but storytelling and metaphors are no doubt a creative way to make curriculum stick in learner's minds.

Verb Tenses		
Tell us WHEN an action is taking place. There are three simple verb tenses:		
Past An action that already took place	Present An action that is happening right now	Future An action that is going to happen
←	↑	→
Usually, you add –ed to the end of the verb I walk**ed** to the store. He walk**ed** to the store. She walk**ed** to the store.	You add –s to the verb for he, she, and it. I walk to the store. He walk**s** to the store. She walk**s** to the store.	You add will before the verb. I **will** walk to the store. He **will** walk to the store. She **will** walk to the store.

    3. Acronyms (as mnemonic devices)

When instructing students, it is common to use acronyms as a mnemonic device, especially when giving lists of information that can be easily memorized through a simple word or sentence. The word or sentence for the acronym is often unusual, which aids in memory recall. For example, the 7 conjunctions in English are often referred to with the word (or invented word) FANBOYS:

F	**A**	**N**	**B**	**O**	**Y**	**S**
o	n	o	u	r	e	o
r	d	r	t		t	

Acronyms can be also used for vocabulary lists:
    Example: My Very Excited Mother Just Served Us Nine Pies (Mercury, Venus, Mars, Jupiter, Saturn, Uranus, Neptune, Pluto)
To aid in difficult spelling:
    Example for the word RHYTHM: Rhythm Helps Your Two Hips Move
And to elucidate grammatical rules:
    Example: I before E except after C, or when sounding like A as in *neighbor* and *weigh*

Certainly creating an acronym can be a fun and creative process for a teacher, and it is not uncommon for teachers to allow students to come up with acronyms themselves.

4. Illustrations (Explicit and Inductive)

One of the most common activities for instruction is the use of an illustration. Often, an instructor will explain a principle or concept, illustrate that concept with examples or illustrations, and then follow up with a question and answer period.

For example, a teacher might teach about the past tense, and instruct on the difference between regular and irregular verbs in the past. After teaching the rules of both regular and irregular, the teacher might provide examples (such as a letter that the teacher wrote). Then the teacher might ask students to identify which verbs were regular or irregular as a sort of assessment activity.

This is a very simple explicit strategy, and is often referred to as the "teach, model, question" strategy (also known as "teach, model, and apply"). While simple, it is often done poorly by either giving too few examples, too many examples, or not enough clarity in the instruction for success.

In a variation on this illustration activity, however, the instructor might wish to NOT present instructions or rules of any kind at first, rather *first* provide models and ask students to come up with the rules on their own. In this variation, students are given time to examine the models and come up with their own assumptions about the rule or rules. This is an inductive strategy, and is often referred to as the "model, infer, elaborate" strategy. This strategy of providing illustrations *first* can be met with some success because it allows students to critically think about the rule rather than simply being told what the rule is. See the example of an inductive activity on articles "a" and "an" below.

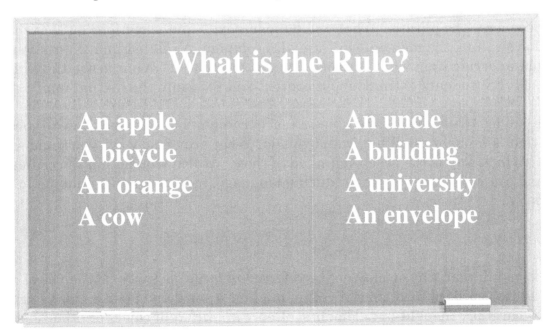

5. Question and Answer

While the question and answer format was discussed briefly as a part of teacher talk, it is an activity that deserves attention on its own. When presenting instruction, it is important to know how and when to ask questions. Questions can be used for a variety of reasons, and each reason will help you determine a time and place for their appropriate to use. While there are many question types, here are a few common types in TESOL instruction.

Quick response or recall: Some questions, such as, "What does 'bicycle' mean?" or "What were the three words we learned yesterday?" are simple questions meant to help students recall information quickly. These kinds of questions should be used sparingly since they often don't engage learners to participate in discussions.

Open Ended Questions: Some questions elicit multiple responses, such as "Who is the best soccer player in the world? Why do you think that?" or "What do you like about camping?" In these questions there is no one correct response, and thus it elicits real conversation and discussion. It also allows for follow up questions, and for students to validate/justify their choices.

"Come on" Questions: Some of the best questions take impossible positions in order to tease out never considered possibilities. Questions like, "Is pollution always bad?" "When should you not tell the truth?" "Should everyone really be treated equally? When should people NOT be treated equally?" These kinds of questions are the dangerous kinds of questions that open up inquisitive thought and critical thinking. Advanced students are able to not only respond with a lot of English content, but can engage in academic skills. While students might say, "Come on!" to such impossible positions, you can tease and intrigue them to think in ways they may not have considered before.

Prediction and Inference Questions: Common in TESOL circles is the use of prediction to intrigue learners. The phrase, "What will happen next?" and variations on that theme, "Where do you think the man will go?" are also common. A related line of questioning comes from inferring from what is read. Why did she do that? What is she thinking? These questions invite students to think about context and read into the textual implications.

Soliciting Advice Questions: Many times a teacher might ask a learner how to solve a problem that is brought up. What would you do? What are three ways you could solve this situation? Which way is the best? Again, all of these involve students in the critical thinking process and are useful not only in producing language, but in inviting students to respond academically.

6. Board Work

Another key skill that may or may not be referred to as an "activity" is the use of a chalk board or white board. Skilled teachers often put board work up before a class starts so that it contains carefully thought-out elements, often with different colors or other features to help items stand out (underlining, bolding, etc.) Teachers use boards not only to write down items, but to draw simple figures and drawings.

For example, when teaching the difficult to understand prepositions, "in, on, and at," one teacher demonstrated that there is a certain degree of specificity that each preposition has in regards to location and time (although there are exceptions that are almost idiomatic in nature, such as "at night," and "in the morning").

For example, "at" is the most specific, and refers not only to a specific moment in time (at 2 pm, at 3:30), but also a specific place (at 234 Chestnut, at my house). "On" can be a bit broader with regards to time (on Wednesday, on January 12th) and location (on the street, on campus), and "in" is broader still with time (in May, in 2012) and location (in the city, in Israel). All of this can be illuminating to students, but representing these concepts visually using board work can have an even greater effect (see illustration below). The use of colors to distinguish between location and time could add even greater clarity.

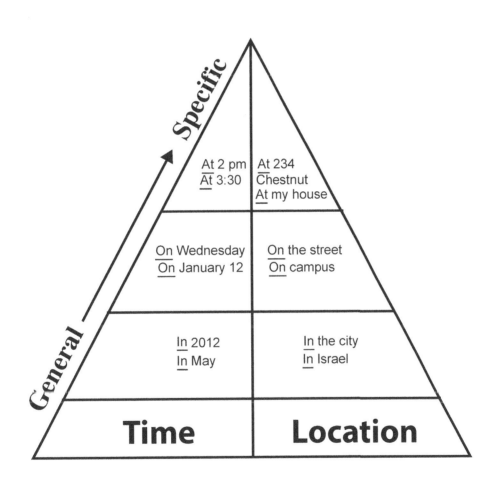

7. Traditional Modeling

A typical model attempts to show an "ideal" example of language production, either written or spoken. Models tend to highlight good English at any level, and also show patterns that students can use to create their own discourse.

For example, when teaching in-text citations to students, you will eventually want to show them a proper model of an in-text citations (and more than one is preferable). In a superior model, you will highlight and illuminate the different sections of a proper citation. Notice in the example below that the model demonstrates not only what the teacher is expecting in terms of content, but demonstrates the different "moves" within the instruction. This teacher wants students to 1. Introduce the quote, 2. Include a partial summary or quote, and then 3. Elaborate on the quote/summary.

Read this model citation. It contains three parts. Read each part and discuss. How do the part differ? How do they support each other?

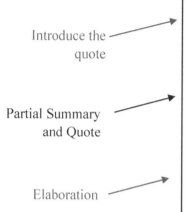

Introduce the quote

Partial Summary and Quote

Elaboration

While some researchers have suggested that most students have an initial "honeymoon stage," culture shock can be very difficult right from the beginning. For example, Bedar Aziz's story "Fifty-five Hours" tells of a young man's struggles even as he is entering the country. He has trouble with airplanes, taxi cabs, trains, and buses. He couldn't understand how to do simple tasks, and states, "My laptop was dying. I looked for a plug. Even the outlets were different here. Why didn't I know that? Another thing I should have known" (2015). Like Aziz, perhaps the most surprising culture shock comes with small details that are different. While people expect to struggle with food and being away from family, most are unprepared to realize that they cannot perform simple tasks that they have done hundreds of times in their own country.

Modeling is often paired with the guided activity referred to as backward fading, which will be explained in the following section.

Guided and Less-Guided Practices

Guided practice comes from a theoretical principle which suggests that, generally, students can't simply do precisely what a teacher says immediately after the teacher says it. Students need time to consider, process, and practice skills that you have invited them to master. Guided practice often takes a portion of a complete, independent activity and has students work on a particular portion of that larger activity. For example, instead of working on an entire essay, students in a guided practice might work on paragraph writing. Similarly, students working on irregular verbs might focus attention on only a few irregular verbs (all with a similar pattern), and then go on to another set of verbs (with another pattern).

Guided practice often takes shape as either teacher-led activities or group-directed activities, but in either case, the activities are structured to break down more difficult tasks. In teacher-led activities, it is wise to invite a variety of students to contribute. This can be done through question and answer, or even by beginning a sentence and inviting students to finish the sentence. Thus, in teacher-led events, you are often the language production "starter" and learners are the language production finishers. While trailing off may sound like a technique of an absent-minded professor, it is, in fact, a technique to engage students and allow them to both predict and create language. In group-directed activities, select groups carefully by ensuring high and low performers in each task. In this configuration, ensure that low performers are given the more difficult task. Studies have shown that when low performers are given the more difficult task, interactivity increases and allows for better overall performance within a group.

Guided activities should, ideally, invite students to think critically about the instruction and give them the requisite time to understand the instruction. A critical goal for guided practice is to get learners to a point where they can perform an independent task, or at the very least feel comfortable attempting one.

1. Backwards Fading (Faded Work Problems)

This guided activity works well especially when inviting students to perform large language production activities such as an essay or a speech. This activity begins with a typical model. For example, below we demonstrate a faded work problem approach to teaching in-text citations to students. Notice in this model that not only an example of an in-text citation is given, but the text is highlighted to illuminate the different sections of a proper citation. In the example given, the model demonstrates not only what the teacher is expecting in terms of content, but demonstrates the different "moves" within the instruction itself. This teacher wants students to 1. Introduce the quote, 2. Include a partial summary or quote, and then 3.

Elaborate on the quote/summary.

Read this model citation. It contains three parts. Read each part and discuss. How do the part differ? How do they support each other?

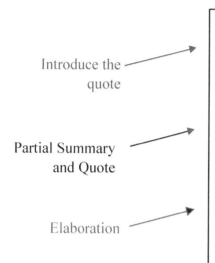

While some researchers have suggested that most students have an initial "honeymoon stage," culture shock can be very difficult right from the beginning. For example, Bedar Aziz's story "Fifty-five Hours" tells of a young man's struggles even as he is entering the country. He has trouble with airplanes, taxi cabs, trains, and buses. He couldn't understand how to do simple tasks, and states, "My laptop was dying. I looked for a plug. Even the outlets were different here. Why didn't I know that? Another thing I should have known" (2015). Like Aziz, perhaps the most surprising culture shock comes with small details that are different. While people expect to struggle with food and being away from family, most are unprepared to realize that they cannot perform simple tasks that they have done hundreds of times in their own country.

A technique that is often paired with modeling is called backwards fading. In this technique, a model is given in steps, but with each new model, learners are given a chance to practice doing one, but not all, of the steps. This allows students to practice using parts of a model until they can practice the complete process on their own. Notice below that this model contains the three steps mentioned in the previous model (introduce the quote, summary/quote, and elaboration), but the student is asked to provide elaboration alone.

Practice: Now finish this model by completing the final step in the citation process.

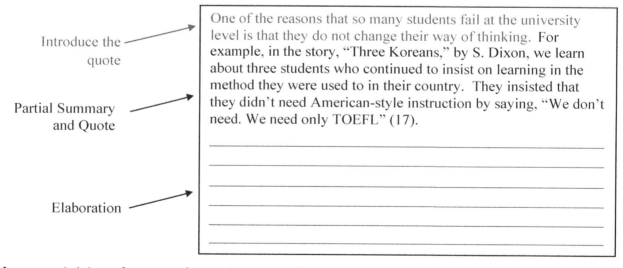

In later activities, the second step is removed (see below) and then finally (not shown), all steps are removed.

Practice: Now finish this model by completing the last two steps in the process.

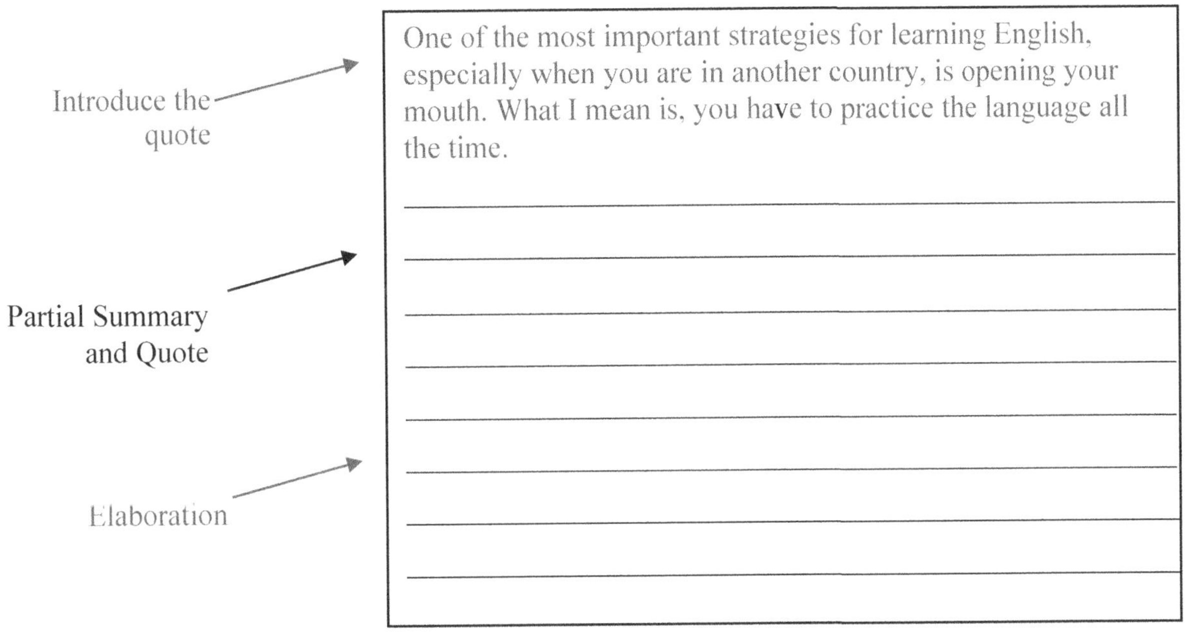

Introduce the quote → One of the most important strategies for learning English, especially when you are in another country, is opening your mouth. What I mean is, you have to practice the language all the time.

Partial Summary and Quote →

Elaboration →

2. The 10-question Salute

Ask 10 questions related to a subject. Students stand and salute after responding to a question. The teacher will "salute" back if the answer is correct. The student may sit down after answering a question correctly. If saluting is considered culturally insensitive, another action can be used in its place, such as a thumbs up or a high five. As a guided practice, these questions should lead students to a better understanding of the instruction and prepare them for an independent activity.

3. Alphabet Soup

Put letters on the board (A-Z, or as many as you'd like). Ask learners to complete each letter with a word or sentence. The words they choose should relate to the topic that they have just learned. For example, if they have just finished watching a video talking about the Serengeti, they could complete the following chart with sentences using the vocabulary and content of the video:

A: Antelopes run wild in the Serengeti.
B: Because they are killers, lions are called the kings of the jungle.
C: Cheetahs run faster than lions.
D: Danger is everywhere on the plains.
E: Elephants use their tusks to fight off predators.
F: Flies swarm the hippos.

You can alter instructions to suit the level of the students. For example, you don't have to require a sentence to begin with the letter (for the letter E, maybe "I love elephants" is an acceptable sentence). This activity helps students to think about what they have recently learned or understood, and gives them a chance to show their learning, and works well especially for a quiz or test.

4. Fill-in-the-blank Questioning

Begin sentences but then trail off and allow learners to complete sentences. This activity can be used to see if students have understood instruction such as a reading or dialogue.

Questions might be about:

> Character: "So the name of the lady was..."
> Place: "And she lived in..."
> Detail: "She didn't want to dance with Ivan because..."
> Inference: "She probably thinks Ivan is..."

When teaching activities such as vocabulary, you can begin sentences with:

> Definitions: I love to climb trees and eat bananas. I am a...
> The word: Monkeys are...
> An antonym: The opposite of day is...

When teaching grammar, you can begin sentences with:

> An example: (give me an example of past tense)

>> The girl...
>> The boy...
>> The elephant and the mouse...

> A Rule/Rules: I am a tense. I like the words always and never. I am...

5. Up Down

Invite students to stand up. Ask questions to any student in the room. Other students must pay attention because, after the first student has given a reply to the question, you will call on a second student to repeat the answer that the first student volunteered. A third student can be required to agree or disagree with the statement spoken by the first and second students. All three students can be seated if they follow the orders correctly and have correct answers.

Independent Practices

Independent practices are simple in concept. The idea is that students have been given instruction, have gone through a number of activities, and are now ready to show their understanding. While independent practice is sometimes seen as an assessment activity, they are not always one and the same. An independent practice may or may not be assessed by a teacher for a final score. Often, an independent activity can serve as the precursor to a test, final presentation, or project.

One of the difficulties for teachers in creating independent activities is that often they take a rather ordinary shape: essay, test, or speech. While each of these devices can be important techniques to allow students to practice their language production, independent activities can extend beyond these typical structures. In project based curriculum, researchers ask teachers to think outside the traditional box and think of unusual and fascinating ways to engage learners in language production.

The following activities attempt to introduce proper use of traditional independent practices, and then demonstrate activities that, with a little creativity from a teacher, might provide engagement and authentic language production where there might otherwise have been a lack of interest from participants.

1. Tests

While a test or examination is something every teacher is familiar with, tests are constructs that are often more difficult to create and administer than many believe. In some sense, bad tests are easy to give, but tests that actually measure knowledge are more complex. Here are a few things to keep in mind:

   a. Ensure that tests measure the right construct. A teacher must have in mind what a student should actually know and be able to perform. A proper test should measure the ability for that student to demonstrate knowledge of the construct. Thus, if the ability to use the passive voice is important for a teacher, a test on identifying the passive voice is NOT going to measure a student's ability in usage.
   b. Ensure that tests measure more than memory. A teacher should also have in mind the idea that a test, in particular a language test, should not just measure the memorization of facts but measure the ability for a student to use language in real situations and in real time.
   c. Teachers who truly want to learn about test construction should consider reading literature about how to best construct a test. Make sure you pay attention to the terms reliability and validity and how they relate to test accuracy.

Multiple choice, true false, fill in the blank, short answer, matching, and other common testing types may or may not be appropriate for language use. Please consider both the strengths and disadvantages of each question type as it relates to the construct you are trying to measure.

2. Compositions

Compositions, or writing essays, are common devices that demonstrate learners' abilities to develop an idea through a writing process. Generally speaking, modern writing theory suggests that essay writing is done over time, with multiple drafts, peer review, and conferencing for best results. In short, the concept is that a composition is not a linear process, but a recursive one, meaning that students must revisit their ideas, reorganize, and revise. Good writing assignments will allow students time to engage in that kind of a process, thus, most writing theorists would suggest that teachers have a series of activities that lead up to the turning in of a final paper. Here are a few ideas:

a. With writing essays, an assignment sheet is often given that demonstrates due dates, different activities for pre-writing, writing, and revision. An assignment sheet makes your expectations clear as a teacher.
b. Model essays should certainly be presented at some point in the writing process, but you must consider when you want to show a model. It may be useful to show a model after the initial brainstorming and first rough draft. Alternatively, some teachers will actually create a model with students as a guided practice activity.
c. When presenting a model, make sure that models demonstrate the types of language you want students to produce. Highlighting or underlining certain writing features in an essay can help students notice the language features you are most interested in having them produce.
d. In addition to presenting a highlighted model, consider using a rubric that identifies key categories that you will use to evaluate the final product.
e. When inviting students to write essays, consider a variety of genres that may prove useful for students in later academic studies (persuasive, descriptive, expository, narrative, investigative, and so forth).

3. Presentations

A presentation is an opportunity for students to demonstrate their ability to speak, present clear and organized ideas, and to show their persuasive or informative power to an audience. This skill also allows students to practice language strategies such as preparing notes and ideas, monitoring language output, organizing information, and controlling anxiety, all important skills for language production. A presentation may be of varied lengths and complexities, but generally have the following elements:

a. As with a writing assignment, a teacher should generally give students clear directions through an assignment sheet. The assignment sheet should clarify the length, topic, and expectations of the speech. Visual elements such as a PowerPoint, pictures, or poster board should also be clearly explained.

b. While a PowerPoint is a common tool, be careful to have students write text that would supplant their ability to speak freely. Speaking production should be natural, and written text should not interfere or replace the majority of the students' speech. In other words, don't turn a presentation into a writing assignment by letting students read their speech!
c. Use of a model and rubric is highly recommended. If you can record past student presentations and demonstrate how they would score on a rubric, this can be an excellent way of demonstrating teacher expectations. Rubric categories vary among language professionals, but may include: organization, use of key vocabulary, pronunciation, body and voice, persuasion, ability to respond to an audience, and use of visual aids.

4. Create and Perform a Dialogue

Inviting students to create and perform a dialogue allows for student creativity and helps learners recognize the use of language in real-life scenarios. It also gives students a chance to interact, negotiate, and conceptualize an audience. When inviting students to create a dialogue ensure that you demonstrate at least one strong model. Also, since dialogue is performed in teams, you may wish students to create the dialogue in teams as well, thus inspiring a collaborative design process. Dialogues need not have all the structure of a proper composition or presentation, but should at the least come with a basic understanding of time limits, use of props, and language forms to be expected.

5. Dramatization

Asking students to dramatize a reading can be one of the most exciting activities a language class can produce. A school production of a short story, for example, might transform a 2-week unit into an exciting theatrical display of language and entertainment. While a dramatization might be done in small groups, some language teachers use them as an opportunity for students to self-select into groups such as the writing team (writes the script), the actors (perform the script), the set designers (create the costumes and set design), and producers (work to promote the production, get an audience, create advertising). When done correctly, this activity promotes real language use and gets students involved in a way that is quite unique.

6. Impromptu Speech

Give learners a chance to show their language production on the spot. Have them choose a topic and speak on that topic for a certain period of time. The impromptu speech is best accomplished when students are given a certain number of phrases they are required to use. While this is often an assignment that is best ungraded, it gives students a chance to demonstrate their instant knowledge of a topic or subject, and instant feedback from a teacher and other learners.

7. Newsletter

Having students create a newsletter as a class can be an exciting opportunity to transform classroom learners into journalists. Students can all be given an opportunity to contribute to the newsletter's different sections. Students might be selected (or select themselves) to write feature stories, sports articles, entertainment or food reviews, get-to-know-you pages (they can interview someone from the school), and even the horoscope. When a teacher assigns this kind of a project, again, models of real life newsletters and newspapers can serve to guide the writing expected.

8. Interviews and Student Presentations

Students may interview someone (another student, a teacher, and so forth) on a particular theme and then present results to the class.

9. Onomatopoeia Scavenger Hunt

Invite students to look for specific words or sounds in real life. Provide a sheet wherein students are given a list of definitions and will be sent out the door in an attempt to get people to think of words that might work. This works really well with onomatopoeia (words that sound like the things they describe). For example, students are required to have someone come up with the "word that describes the sound a dog makes" or "the sound of a bird." When my students do this activity, they need to be careful and make sure they find a word (bark) and not just a sound (bow-wow).

10. Commercials/Advertisements

You can record commercials on tape or have students simply perform their commercials by creating products that have something to do with the theme.
If you have access to a video camera you can record the student commercials and then watch them in class the following day. Have the students evaluate an aspect of the commercial (for example: Was the commercial visually appealing? How did they make their commercial visually appealing?)

11. Class Field Trip

Take learners to a baseball game if you are learning about baseball. Take them to the local newspaper if you are writing news reports. To make it a proper independent practice, invite students to write or speak about what they learned.

Part III: Templates/Activity Resource

The following templates are meant to help teachers generate ideas of their own and have a clearer picture of the TESOL activities explained in the previous two sections. As every classroom may differ in level, age, and culture, these are not necessarily for use in every classroom, but are intended to demonstrate common material.

Please note that included in this section is a sample one-week planning guide (page 31 and 32) that follows the activities included herein. New teachers are encouraged to make copies of this planning guide and follow it in their classroom preparation. The guide can help remind teachers in a whole language classroom to do the following:

1. Keep a balance of reading, writing, listening, and speaking activities.
2. Keep a log that demonstrates the use of proper warm-ups, instruction, controlled (guided) practices, and less controlled (independent) practices.
3. Keep a convenient record of materials that will be used in the next classes.
4. Keep track of homework, the collection of journals or logs, and so forth.

This lesson plan is not meant to replace any school mandated lesson plan structure that a teacher might use, but rather demonstrates what a lesson plan might have. The use of the one-week lesson plan versus a one-day lesson plan is for convenience only.

Cloze Passage

"Scarborough Fair"
(English Folk Song)

Directions: This song is a traditional love song often sung by a man asking a woman to do impossible things, followed by a woman asking a man to do impossible things. As you listen, please fill in the words from the blanks. When the song is over, talk to a partner and answer the following questions: Why would people who love each other ask for the impossible?

(Man)

Are you going to Scarborough (1) _____?
Parsley, sage, rosemary, and thyme.
Remember me to one who lives there.
She once was a true love of mine.
Tell her to make me a cambric (2) _____.
Parsley, sage, rosemary, and thyme.
Without no seam nor (3) _____.
Then she'll be a (4) _____ love of mine.

(Woman)

Tell him to find me an acre of (5) _____.
Parsley, sage, rosemary, and thyme.
Between the salt water and the sea (6) _____.
Then he'll be a true love of mine.
Are you going to Scarborough (1) _____?
Parsley, sage, rosemary, and thyme.
Remember me to one who lives there.
He once was a (4) _____ love of mine.

Vocabulary answers

1. Fair
2. shirt
3. needlework
4. true
5. land
6. Stand

How to Make a Group

Directions: Give one card to each member of a group of three. For larger groups, consider creating other responsibilities such as timekeeper (someone who monitors and informs the group about time remaining) and informant (someone who sees what other groups are doing and saying). All group members should be active participants in sharing ideas and performing the activity.

Group Leader

Job description: Help the group follow the instructions for the activity. Does everyone understand what to do? Help them understand. Make sure each member of the group has a chance to speak about the task. Don't do all the talking, but instead lead the group to complete the activity with equal participation from each member.

Secretary

Job description: Help the group by taking notes on what is discussed. Keep your notes simple. Give the main ideas of what is talked about. Important!! Write your notes so that another person can read what you write. Summarize. The group members will help you decide exactly what to write if you aren't sure.

Reporter

Job description: You have two jobs. (1) Help the group by keeping track of the time for the activity. The teacher will give the time limit. It's your responsibility to warn the group when time is nearly at an end. (2) After your group finishes, you will tell the whole class about your group discussion. You must use the secretary's notes to help you speak about the work that your group did together. When it's your turn, stand up and speak for your group. Speak for 2-3 minutes.

Half-Reading

Part 1 Directions: Read this article and answer the questions provided below. Then read the full article and see how well you were able to infer the answers.

> **Questions 1-2 are based
> passage.**
>
> Early scientists beli
> dinosaurs, like most repti
> immediately abandoned
> hatched young were left
> themselves. However, th
> group of nests has challe
> nests, which contained fc
> dinosaurs that were not u
> dence that dinosaur parei
> their young. For some tir
> babies stayed at the nest
> brought back plant matte
> stayed at home until they
> roam safely on their own

1. What did scientists used to believe about dinosaurs?
2. What did the newly hatched young have to do?
3. What do scientists believe now about dinosaurs?

Part 2 Directions: Your teacher will now read the full text. After listening to the teacher, discuss with your partner what you heard and revise your answers according to what you hear.

> **Questions 1-2 are based on the following passage.**
>
> Early scientists believe that all dinosaurs, like most reptiles, laid and then immediately abandoned their eggs. The newly hatched young were left to take care of themselves. However, the recent discovery of a group of nests has challenged this belief. The nests, which contained fossilized baby dinosaurs that were not unborn, provided evidence that dinosaur parents actually cared for their young. For some time after birth, the babies stayed at the nest while the parents brought back plant matter for food. The young stayed at home until they were large enough to roam safely on their own.

Reader's Outline

Directions: As you read, look for three or more main ideas. Under each main idea, what are the subtopics under each idea? And under the sub-topics, are there points and even more points the author makes? Use the following outline provided below to write an outline of the reading.

Heading:
1. Main Topic
    a. Sub Topic
        i. points under the subtopic
        ii. more points
        iii. even more points
    b. Sub Topic 2
        i. points under the subtopic
        ii. more points
        iii. even more points
2. Main Topic 2
    a. Sub Topic
        i. points under the subtopic
        ii. more points
        iii. even more points
    b. Sub Topic 2
        i. points under the subtopic
        ii. more points
        iii. even more points
3. Main Topic 3
    a. Sub Topic
        i. points under the subtopic
        ii. more points
        iii. even more points

Character Map

Directions: Choose a character. Find three characteristics that are worth exploring. Find examples to support each of the characteristics you have chosen.

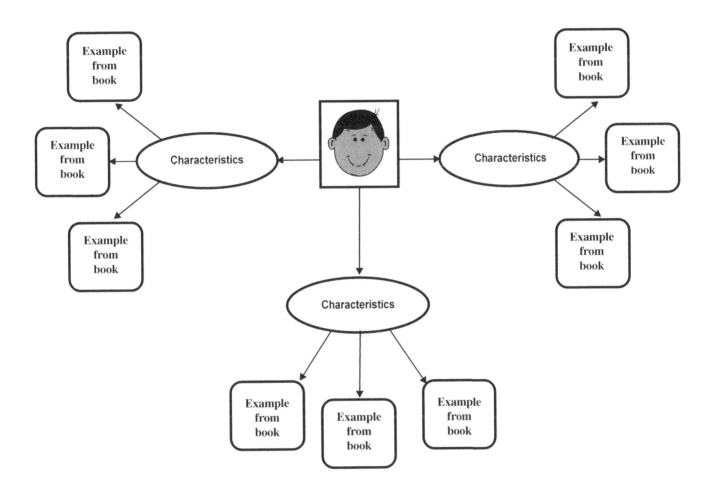

TESOL Mapp

Directions for a Reading: After reading a story, think of the main idea, supporting details, and purpose of the story. Then write your own personal reaction to the story. (Example based on the story, "No Speak English" from the *House on Mango Street*, by Sandra Cisneros.)

Main Idea	Analysis of Supporting Details
To show the difficulties of a working immigrant's wife and her barriers to learn English and fit in.	1. Doesn't leave the house 2. Complains to husband 3. Sings songs from her country 4. Looks at pictures 5. Tries to stop boy from speaking English
Purpose	**Personal Reaction**
To inform us to understand a situation, to make us feel compassion for Mamacita	*I liked this story a lot. It made me want to visit Mamacita and give her some advice.*

Main Idea	Analysis of Supporting Details
Purpose	**Personal Reaction**

Rank Order Exercise

Directions: While you are reading, write down the ideas that seem most important to you. After you finish reading, decide which ideas are most important or most interesting. Put the most important or interesting point first, then the second, third, fourth, and so on. Be prepared to discuss why you put these ideas in this order.

Ideas	Ranking (order of importance or interest)
	1
	2
	3
	4
	5
	6

73

Example of a Cluster/Brainstorm

Directions: A proper cluster can guide an entire essay by organizing a thesis statement (pictured in the center) with subtopics branching out from the main idea, and details or evidences to support each subtopic. The cluster below is a textual analysis of the anti-war song "Russians."

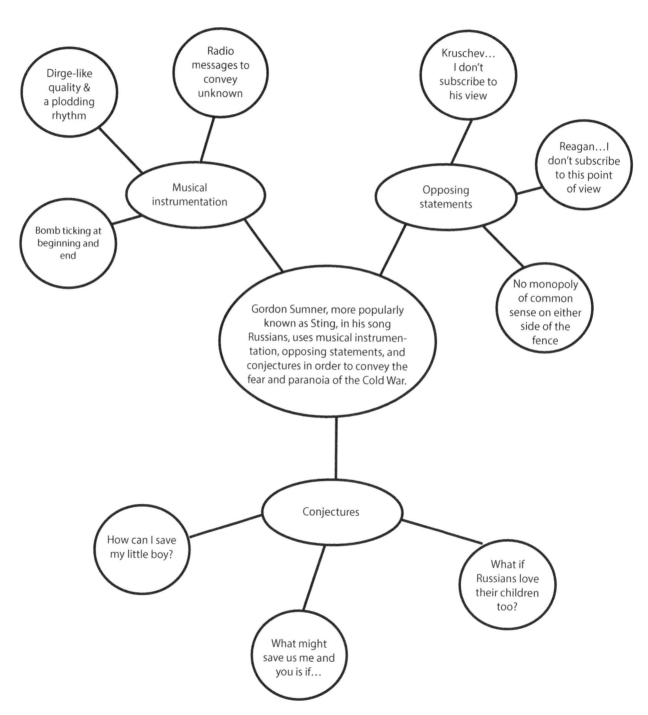

Example of a Venn Diagram

Directions: Put things that relate to one topic in one circle, things that relate to another topic in another circle, and things that they share in common at the intersection.

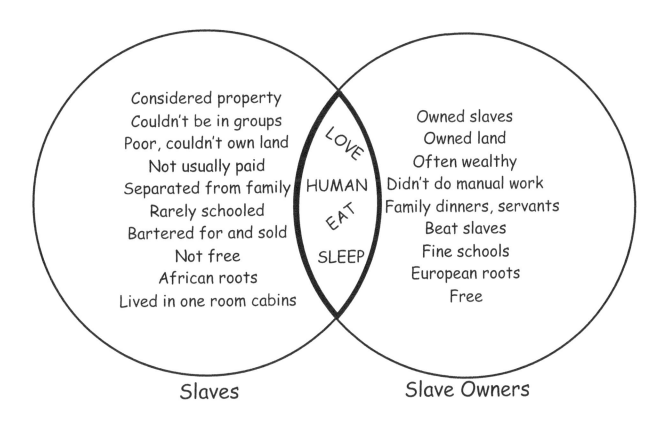

Draw a Picture

Directions for the Teacher: Ask students to get out a piece of paper. Or, ask one student to read and another student to draw. The student who reads must not show the reading to the other student. You may tell the students that you want to see how close their drawing is to one that you are looking at. For more advanced students, invite them to ask questions (Where are the windows? Where is the door?)

Directions for the Student: Draw a VERY large circle on your paper. Inside the circle, draw a small house. There are two windows and a door. Put a chimney on top of the roof. There is smoke coming out of the chimney. Draw the smoke. Behind the house is a tree. Now draw a man who is at the top of the tree. He is waving and smiling. Does your picture look like mine?

Value Lines

Directions: Your teacher will give some statements. Mark how much you agree with each statement by marking an x on the line, or circle the face if you **completely** disagree or agree.

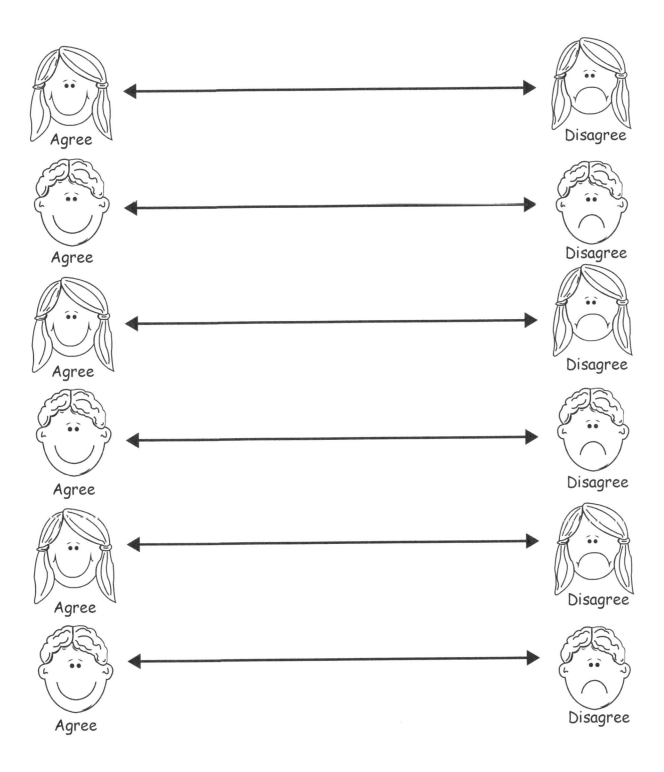

More Than Name Tags

Directions for teachers: On the first day of class (or perhaps a day when the class introduces themselves to a new student), cut out enough name tags for each student. Have students fasten these to their chests with a pin or tape and walk around the class sharing each idea. As an extension activity, students may have to memorize a partner's nametag and introduce the partner to the whole class.

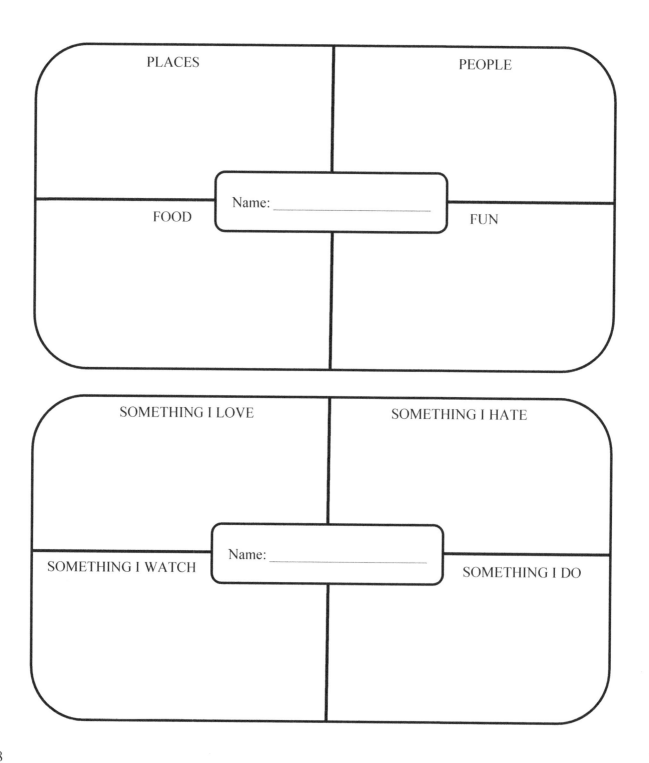

Find Someone Who…

Directions: Find classmates to sign the categories you see listed. You may write the name of a classmate on only one line. The winner is the first person to have all the categories signed!

Find someone who…

1. Has a short name: _____
2. Has a long name: _____
3. Has a famous name: _____
4. Loves to cook: _____
5. Has a pet: _____
6. Plays a musical instrument: _____
7. Likes to sing: _____
8. Has a celebrity crush: _____
9. Has an unusual talent: _____
10. Will be famous some day: _____
11. Loves to talk a lot: _____
12. Is very shy: _____
13. Has visited more than 3 countries: _____
14. Can play a sport competitively: _____
15. Loves this class: _____
16. Doesn't like fruit: _____
17. Loves to read: _____
18. Hates cell phones: _____
19. Had a dream last night: _____
20. Has more than 3 brothers and sisters: _____

Sentence Starters: What's My Line?

Directions: Finish as many sentences as you can. Your teacher may call on you or you may be asked to speak in a group.

1. I was very happy the time I…
2. My face has a big smile when…
3. I hate to eat…
4. I would not like to live without…
5. I wish I could…
6. I like my…
7. I like to pretend I…
8. I would like a great big…
9. It's hard for me to…
10. On Saturdays, I like to…
11. I feel silly when…
12. I'm sure glad I…
13. Sometimes I'm afraid of…
14. I always feel good when…
15. I once got hurt when…
16. When I grow up, I…
17. I'm pretty good at…
18. I hate it when…
19. At school, I like to…
20. I wish people would stop…
21. I like the sound of…
22. I feel sad when…
23. At school I like to…
24. My family likes to…
25. I am afraid to…
26. I laugh when…
27. Two of my favorite things are…
28. I don't like to…
29. Once someone helped me by…
30. I would hate to lose…
31. I love to give…
32. I hope that…
33. I would like to learn how to…
34. If I were a giant, I would…
35. I really like…
36. What really bothers me is…
37. I'll never forget…
38. I would hate to lose…
39. I love to give…
40. I'd like to say a good thing about…
41. I like to play…
42. I was really scared once when…
43. I like the way I…
44. Two things I like about myself are…
45. I sometimes get mad when….
46. I would not like to have…
47. I feel happiest when…
48. I feel bad when…
49. I would like a magic ring that…
50. I feel important when…

Balanced and Integrated Lesson Guide   Instructor: _____

ActivityCount–Report	Day 1	Day 2	Day 3	Day 4	Day 5
How many activities of each skill that you completed this week. Listening: Speaking: Reading: Writing:					
Materials Needed Support materials for each day's lesson					

81

Reading	Writing	Listening	Speaking
Predict from a Title Story Guesswork Jigsaw Question Jigsaw Find a Word, Find a Sentence Reading with Half the Words Reader's Outline Character Map Reading Log Scrambled Sentences Picture Books Focus on Organization Skits on Reading Focus on a Literary Technique Mapping Summarizing/Paraphrase Picture the Story Rank Order Exercise Alphabet Reading	Workstations Free-writing Fast-writing Clustering/Brainstorming Venn Diagrams Unfinished Stories Any 4 Pictures Make a Story Guesswork Dictation Remember the Picture Draw Your Neighborhood Journals Poetry Writing	The Missing Half Headbands Back to Back 20 Question Quiz Truth or Fiction Cloze Passage Draw a Picture Perform the Instruction (Fetch It!) Dictation Secret Orders Story with Mistakes Guest Speaker	Picture Prompt This Makes Me Think That… Circle Speaking Interaction Lines Agree/Disagree Value Lines Story Chain Ghost Stories in the Dark Folktale Storytelling Discussion Questions Fishbowl Three Objects in a Backpack

Sample Class Structure for an Integrated Classroom

	Day 1	Day 2	Day 3	Day 4	Day 5
Week 1	Reading Task Focused Speaking Begin Literature	Writing Task Focused Listening Literature, continued	Reading Task Focused Speaking Finish Literature	Writing Task Focused Listening Study Vocabulary	Turn in journals Check Logs Review/Catch-up
Week 2	Reading Task Focused Speaking Composition Rough draft due	Writing Task Focused Listening Vocabulary Game	Reading Task Focused speaking Vocabulary activity Composition due	Writing Task Focused listening Vocabulary Test	Check logs Turn in journals Testing

Made in the USA
Las Vegas, NV
27 June 2024

91575277R00046